HOME OFFICE RESEARCH STUDY No. 134

Contacts between Police and Public:
findings from the 1992 British Crime Survey

by Wesley G. Skogan

A HOME OFFICE
RESEARCH AND PLANNING UNIT
REPORT

LONDON: HMSO

ISBN 0 11 341115 4

HOME OFFICE RESEARCH STUDIES

'Home Office Research Studies' comprise reports on research undertaken in the Home Office to assist in the exercise of its administrative functions, and for the information of the judicature, the services for which the Home Secretary has responsibility (direct or indirect) and the general public.

On the last pages of this report are listed titles already published in this series, in the preceding series *Studies in the Causes of Delinquency and the Treatment of Offenders,* and in the series of *Research and Planning Unit Papers.*

HMSO

Standing order service

Placing an order with HMSO BOOKS enables a customer to receive other titles in this series automatically as published.

This saves time, trouble and expense of placing individual orders and avoids the problems of knowing when to do so.

For details please write to HMSO BOOKS (PC11B.2), Publications Centre, PO Box 276, London SW8 5DT and quoting reference 25.-08.011.

The standing order service also enables customers to receive automatically as published all material of their choice which additionally saves extensive catalogue research. The scope and selectivity of the service has been extended by new techniques, and there are more than 3,500 classifications to choose from. A special leaflet describing the service in more detail may be obtained on request.

Foreword

Concerns about public attitudes towards the police are reflected at the present time in the police service's Quality of Service Programme. Customer expectations of policing, and the reactions of the public to the services they received from the police are of interest at both national and local levels. Police forces themselves are monitoring local public attitudes on a regular basis, while surveys such as the British Crime Survey provide a valuable opportunity to do the same thing nationally.

This report presents further findings from the 1992 British Crime Survey. It examines the whole range of contacts that people have with the police, whether or not these are related to crime. This is the fourth sweep of the BCS to look at public attitudes towards the police, and the report compares data over time from the BCS and other surveys showing trends in public satisfaction with policing. The second part of the report considers the factors that determine whether victims report crimes to the police, and their views about the response they receive when they do so.

ROGER TARLING

Head of the Research and Planning Unit

May 1994

Acknowledgements

I would like to thank Natalie Aye Maung for her assistance and guidance in working with the BCS data, Pat Mayhew and Peter Martin for their patient review of several drafts of this report, and Peter Southgate for his attention to both the details of the report and the larger issues it addresses.

WESLEY G. SKOGAN

Contents

Summary

This report presents some of the findings of the 1992 British Crime Survey (BCS) about people's experiences of and attitudes towards the police. It describes the reasons why people contacted the police, and the circumstances under which the police stopped and questioned members of the public. It also describes what happened during these encounters, and people's assessments of how well the police had done their job. Another chapter examines in detail the factors that lie behind the reporting of crimes to the police.

Public satisfaction

Earlier sweeps of the BCS documented a decline in satisfaction with police performance. To monitor this trend, the Home Office sponsored several more surveys, and the 1992 BCS included a special supplement of questions about the police. As a whole, the surveys show that the general level of public confidence in the police declined modestly between 1988 and 1992: the overall percentage rating their local police as very or fairly good fell from 86 per cent to 81 per cent. But, although earlier surveys showed a steady decline in the number of people rating police performance as very good, this decline appears to have steadied: in 1988 25 per cent said the police were very good, while 24 per cent said so in 1992.

The 1992 BCS also shows that satisfaction among victims with how their cases are handled has rallied a little. Also, the public in general thought that the police made a particularly good job of dealing with crowds, traffic and accidents. But police effectiveness in dealing with burglary, white-collar crime and crime victims was seen much less favourably; and respondents were also less satisfied with foot patrol. Visible police patrols and personal acquaintance with an officer were related to higher levels of satisfaction, as was reliance on the mass media for information about policing.

Contact with the police

In all, 54 per cent of those interviewed had had some encounter with the police during the previous year. About a third of respondents had contacted the police about some matter, 20 per cent had been stopped or investigated in some way, and 14 per cent had been visited by the police rendering them some service. The most notable difference between these rates and those for the 1988 BCS was the frequency with which people had been stopped in vehicles, which had risen from 12 to 16 per cent.

Public dissatisfaction

The survey also documented the frequent dissatisfaction of crime victims and those contacting the police to report a crime. About a third of those who had contacted the police about a crime felt the police had not shown enough interest or given the case enough attention, and only about a quarter felt they had been kept well enough informed. People who had reported suspicious circumstances, disturbances, ringing alarms and nuisances were also often dissatisfied with how their complaint had been handled, and for the same reasons. Like past studies, the 1992 BCS also documented high levels of dissatisfaction among racial minorities and younger people, both with how they had been treated when stopped by the police and when they had asked the police for information, advice or help.

Those who had been stopped by the police generally felt that they had been given good reasons why. They were sanctioned in some way (fined, searched, etc.) in a minority of cases. Most people who had been stopped in vehicles thought they had been treated fairly, but that the police had not shown much interest in what they had had to say on their own behalf.

About one in five people who had been stopped on foot thought they had been treated unfairly. They reported having been treated less politely than those who had contacted the police themselves. But more respondents who had been stopped on foot, compared to those who had called the police about a crime, said they were very or fairly satisfied with how the police had handled this.

Police response to calls

It is also important to note what people were not dissatisfied about, or what did not seem to affect their overall judgements of policing. More than 80 per cent were satisfied with how rapidly the police had responded when they had contacted them, and those who thought they might have come faster were not particularly dissatisfied with how their case as a whole had been handled. Almost no one complained about offenders not having been caught or property not having been recovered.

At least 95 per cent of respondents contacting the police thought they had been treated very politely or fairly politely. Most of the contacts initiated by the public had been handled courteously, as had 80 per cent or more of those initiated by the police. By and large, the police had given what people felt were good reasons for having stopped them. Overtly racist language or behaviour by the police was rare.

Unreported offences

One purpose of the BCS is to examine unreported offences. Surveys of crime victims around the world have shown the "dark figure" of unreported offences to be a substantial one. This report examines factors related to the reporting of crime, and concludes that crime reporting is strongly related to the seriousness of the crime. It is driven by the intrusiveness of the crime, the threat it poses for the personal safety of its victims, the extent of injury and loss it entails, and its emotional impact.

But more than the seriousness of the crime is involved in reporting. Afro-Caribbeans were about six per cent less likely than others to report crimes to the police, no matter what the situation in which they had found themselves and in spite of their tending to have been victims of more serious crimes. Crimes whose perpetrators had some link to their victims (as relatives, partners, friends and neighbours) also often went unreported.

These related-party crimes included a disproportionate number of violent assaults, as well as most crimes causing injury uncovered by the BCS. Eighty per cent of all crimes against the person that had involved people related to one another led to injury. One-third of those victims needed a doctor's attention. Twenty per cent of the victims cited fear of reprisal as the reason for not having reported the violent assault.

An important factor leading less serious crimes to be reported is insurance. The increasing scope of insurance coverage may explain the increasing rates of property crime reporting over the years. Crime reporting was also higher, regardless of its seriousness, among older victims and home owners, both growing sections of the population.

1 Introduction

This report presents those findings of the 1992 British Crime Survey (BCS) that describe people's experiences of the police and their attitudes towards the police. The report describes why people contacted the police and why the police stopped and questioned members of the public. It also describes what happened during those encounters and the assessments people gave of how well the police had done their job.

The Quality of Service Programme

The police service's Quality of Service Programme aims to improve policing in a way that can be seen and, in doing so, to increase public confidence in the police. The effectiveness of the police depends on public confidence. The police need the public to report crimes and other emergencies willingly and quickly. The police also need the public to cooperate in police investigations. Neighbourhood Watch needs the public's support and participation, and such crime prevention schemes will work only if many people take part.

The Quality of Service Programme is partly a response to the decline in confidence repeatedly seen in opinion polls during the 1980s. The Programme is also in the spirit of the Citizen's Charter, which calls for more consumer awareness in the provision of public services.

The Association of Chief Police Officers (ACPO) has identified several areas in which police effectiveness can be monitored by surveying the public. These areas range from the satisfactory management of calls from the public to police consultation of and involvement with the community. Many police forces have been carrying out local surveys to monitor people's attitudes, to help set policing priorities, and to evaluate and fine tune their service to the public.

The findings of the 1992 BCS provide a broader picture of relations between the police and the public, which can serve as a backdrop to local surveys, as well as point to trends. The BCS is large enough to identify national areas of concern in different groups of the population, ranging from people who have had contact with the police to people whose only impression of the police comes from the media.

This report focuses on people who have had contact with the police because those people's experiences and opinions should give a better basis for assessing the police's efforts. The BCS describes the main sources of their satisfaction and dissatisfaction with policing, and points to some strategic directions that local forces might take to help rebuild public confidence.[1]

To assess the views of the public, BCS respondents were asked a series of questions about their backgrounds and their experiences of crime. Half the respondents were then asked an extra set of questions about the police. (The other half were asked about other matters, such as crime prevention, obscene telephone calls, and their attitudes towards sentencing.) Those respondents who had had contact with the police were asked to describe why those encounters had taken place and how often. They were also asked to detail what had happened, and to give their opinions of how they had been treated by the police and of the quality of service they felt they had received.

The BCS also included general questions about how well the police performed various tasks, and about any complaints those respondents had made or had considered making against individual police officers. All crime victims identified in the BCS were asked detailed questions about each incident that had occurred during the previous year. Those questions included whether or not the incident had come to the attention of the police.

This report uses the data to examine several issues. Chapter 2 makes use of 10 years of opinion surveys to examine trends in the public's satisfaction with police performance. Repeated sweeps of the BCS during the 1980s documented an erosion of satisfaction with the police. This chapter extends that series of sweeps into the 1990s, and reports on other survey data tracking trends in opinion. These surveys show that the decline in confidence recorded during the 1980s seems to have stabilised.

Chapter 3 examines the nature of the encounters between the public and the police and what these encounters reveal about the extent of public satisfaction with the service the police provide. These contacts were often not emergencies, simply routine. They also illustrate the diverse nature of police-public contact. The public initiated most of these encounters by dialling 999, by telephoning their local police station, by going to a police station, or by approaching an officer on the street. The police initiated encounters by stopping motorists and people on foot, and by going to people's homes to seek information or to investigate a complaint. Chapter 3 focuses on the relationship between these experiences and people's assessments of how they had been treated.

People's attitudes towards the police have many sources, many of which are difficult to change. Chapters 2 and 3 describe important social and economic differences in attitudes. One source of opinion that can be changed is how people are treated by the police. People's experiences play an important role in shaping popular opinion. The 1992 BCS points to generally high levels of popular satisfaction with the way the police had handled

---

[1] For a discussion of the uses of opinion surveys for evaluating the police, see Hough, 1989.

encounters with the public, but it also identifies practices that undermine support for the police.

Chapter 4 takes a detailed look at the reporting of crimes to the police. Many crimes go unreported. About 43 per cent of crimes were brought to the attention of the police. Compared to earlier sweeps of the BCS, this represents a statistically significant increase in the public's reporting of crime. In the 1982 BCS, the figure was only 31 per cent, and the BCS has documented a steady increase in reporting rates since then. This explains part, but only part, of the subsequent increase in officially recorded crime. (For more details, see Mayhew and Aye Maung, 1992.)

Chapter 4 also examines the factors associated with the reporting of crime. These factors include the degree of injury and loss suffered, how deeply events intruded into victims' private lives and how likely victims were to be compensated for their distress. The 1992 BCS shows that whether or not people reported crimes often depended on what they saw as the costs and benefits of doing so. Factors such as a close relationship between the parties involved tended to stop a significant number of serious crimes from being reported.

The final chapter summarises the research findings and discusses their implications for efforts to increase the quality of service provided by the police.

About the BCS

The 1992 BCS questioned residents of 10,059 randomly selected households in England and Wales. Respondents were chosen to make up a representative cross section of people of 16 years of age and older, living in private households. The sampling frame was the Postcode Address File, which is a national listing of all postal delivery points. It represents the most comprehensive register of household addresses. People living in institutions were not sampled.

An additional sample of Afro-Caribbean and Asian respondents was selected to boost their numbers for the analysis of crime victims. These respondents were not asked the questions on attitudes to policing but their responses are included in the discussion of crime reporting in Chapter 4.

Interviewers from Social and Community Planning Research and British Market Research Bureau conducted the survey. The fieldwork was carried out in January, February and March 1992, and the survey's response rate was 77 per cent. (For a more detailed description of the BCS and the findings of the 1992 survey, see Mayhew et al., 1993.)

The BCS deliberately over sampled inner-city residents because they are more likely to be victims of crime. In the analyses presented in this report, weights were used to adjust the data so that inner–city respondents were counted in their correct proportion. Weights were also used to adjust for the possible under representation, in an addressed-based sample, of people living in households of several adults. Because of these sampling and weighting procedures, conservative tests of statistical significance were used throughout.

2 Public confidence in the police

Introduction

An earlier report based on the 1988 BCS (Skogan, 1990) documented an erosion of public support for the police. Between the first sweep of the BCS in 1982 and the 1988 survey, the percentage of people who rated the performance of their local police as very good dropped from 43 per cent to 25 per cent. When combined with the percentage of people who thought the police did a fairly good job, overall satisfaction declined from 92 per cent to 86 per cent. Independent public opinion polls supported these findings. The widespread nature of this decline in confidence seemed to be another reason for concern. Compared to earlier surveys, the 1988 BCS found that confidence had declined the most in small towns and rural areas, among women and the elderly, among whites and among crime victims. These were groups that were generally considered to be supporters of the police.

This trend was significant because the police depend on the cooperation of the public. The police rely on victims to report crimes quickly and accurately, and rely on witnesses coming forward to help the police investigate those crimes. The police also rely on the public to report accidents and emergencies. In turn, the public expects effective and courteous service from the police.

Much public money is invested in policing and, as consumers of the police service, the public is increasingly concerned to get value for money. Declining public confidence in police performance could hamper police operations and threaten to undermine the consensus that supports the staffing and expenditure levels that maintain the quality of the service.

Trends in public satisfaction

To monitor trends in public opinion more closely, the Home Office commissioned a series of national polls that repeated or adapted some BCS questions about the police. Three of these polls were conducted between the 1988 and 1992 sweeps of the BCS, another was done at about the same time as the 1992 survey, and two were carried out later in 1992. Although these national polls were smaller, and conducted differently from the BCS, the results were similar.

They point to a stabilising of confidence in the police during the late 1980s and early

1990, at or slightly below the 1988 level. (Figure 2.1 presents a summary of these polls; there is a technical discussion of the questions in Appendix A; and more detailed statistical findings are presented in Appendix B.)

Figure 2.1
Ratings of Police Performance by respondents with an opinion

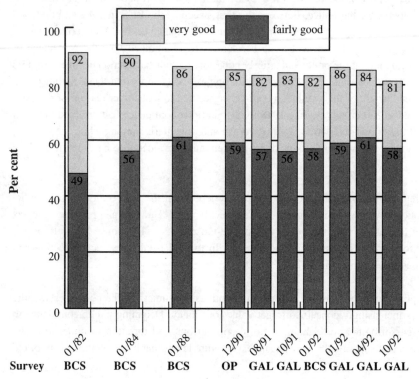

The first of these post-1988 polls was carried out by the Office of Population Censuses and Surveys (OPCS) in December 1990. The OPCS sample was smaller than the BCS (only about 1,620 people were interviewed), but it used the same sampling frame as the 1992 BCS. Compared to the BCS conducted in early 1988, the OPCS poll found that, among those with an opinion, almost exactly the same percentage of people gave the police very good and fairly good ratings. In early 1988, 25 per cent of the people interviewed thought the police did a very good job and 61 per cent thought the police did a fairly good job. In late 1990, the comparable figures were 26 per cent and 59 per cent. (The OPCS survey is designated "OP" in Figure 2.1.) In that period of almost two years, there was no overall change in the level of public confidence in police.

This stability was confirmed by later surveys conducted by the Gallup organisation. Between August 1991 and October 1992, Gallup conducted five surveys that repeated some BCS questions on the police. Gallup interviewed between 1,840 and 2,000 people each time, but used a quota-based sampling procedure, which yields less precise estimates than the OPCS or BCS. (The results of the Gallup surveys, and the findings of the larger 1992 BCS, are also presented in Figure 2.1 and are respectively labelled "GAL" and "BCS". A thorough discussion of the Gallup surveys is presented in a report by Southgate and Crisp, 1992.)

The latest BCS points to another small drop in public confidence in the police between 1988 and 1992. The overall percentage of people who rated local police work as very good or fairly good, rather than poor, fell from 86 to 82 per cent; this difference is statistically significant. The BCS, with its large and highly representative sample, shows a continuing, albeit modest, downward trend, according to these figures. But the percentage of people who gave police a very good rating remained almost unchanged. That percentage stood at 25 per cent in 1988, and 24 per cent in 1992.

Those figures, and the 26 per cent of people who held a highly favourable view of the police service in the 1990 OPCS survey, are not significantly different from one another. Figure 2.1 illustrates this. Between 1982 and 1992, overall public satisfaction dropped about 3 percentage points at each sweep of the BCS. The more gripping trend in the data has been the decline in the percentage of people giving the police top marks. Beginning in 1982, that figure dropped about nine percentage points at each reading, and was the major focus of reports about policing based on the 1988 BCS. That decline now seems to have stabilised.

The Gallup surveys conducted before and after the 1992 BCS point to the same conclusion. The Gallup poll carried out at about the same time as the 1992 BCS (but using a much smaller and less representative sample) found 27 per cent of those with an opinion rated police performance as very good, compared to 24 per cent in the BCS. Other polls in 1992 set that figure at 23 per cent. Overall, the OPCS, Gallup and BCS surveys since 1988 put the percentage of people rating the police as very good in the 23-to-27 per cent range, which represents a high level of agreement given the disparities in their samples and procedures.

General satisfaction (adding in those who thought the police did a fairly good job) ranged from 81 to 86 per cent. With the exception of the Gallup survey in January 1992, these surveys are all within the sampling error of the 1992 BCS. They confirm the general conclusion that, firstly, the overall level of public confidence in the police declined very modestly between 1988 and 1992; and, secondly, the dramatic decline in the percentage of people giving the police their highest vote of confidence has been stabilised.

This trend is paralleled by the changes in how victims of crime felt the police had handled their cases. Mayhew et al. (1993) examined the perceptions of victims in the 1984, 1988, and 1992 sweeps of the BCS. They found that the decline in satisfaction with the police registered by victims between 1984 and 1988 was partially made up by the more recent increases in satisfaction. Overall, the levels of satisfaction with the police among crime victims interviewed in the most recent BCS remained slightly below the levels of satisfaction felt by people questioned in 1984. But the recovery in public satisfaction was impressive, especially among victims of burglary and vandalism. As the next chapter shows, reporting a crime to the police is one of the most frequent ways in which the public has contact with the police, so this improvement in how people felt the police had handled their cases is potentially very important.

Perceptions of police performance

The 1992 BCS included questions about various aspects of police performance, including respondents' views of how successful they thought the police were at fighting crime, regulating traffic, responding to accidents, relating to the community and controlling public drinking.[1] Table 2.1 presents the distribution of opinion on 13 different aspects of police work. The responses are ranked from high to low, according to the level of public satisfaction. The survey shows fairly high levels of satisfaction with many aspects of police work, but it also points to concern about a few aspects of policing.

It is also apparent that many respondents knew they were not well informed about what the police were doing, which is revealed in the many "don't know" responses to questions about victim support, white-collar crime and community relations. "Don't know" responses were more common from people who had had little recent experience of crime or the police. Respondents who had contacted the police or who had been stopped by them in the past year were more likely to have an opinion about most aspects of policing. The same was true of people who had been victims of crime in the past year. All of these groups were consistently more likely to be negative in their views. About 54 per cent of those interviewed for the BCS had had contact with the police, so the impact of experience was considerable.

Responses to the questions in Table 2.1 can be organised under six headings. The first five are: Patrolling on foot and by car; Fighting crime; Regulating traffic; Relations with the community; and Controlling disorder. In addition, it proves useful to combine the responses to all of them into one global index of opinion.

---

[1] For a description of several successful attempts to cope with problems associated with public drinking, see Ramsay, 1991.

Table 2.1
Ratings of Police Service Delivery

Attitudes Toward Police Service Delivery	Per cent rating police job ...				
	very good	fairly good	fairly poor	very poor	don't know
responding to accidents and medical emergencies	59	31	3	1	6
controlling crowds at sporting and public events	32	47	6	2	12
dealing with serious motoring offences	32	44	12	4	8
giving advice on how to prevent crime	25	42	16	6	11
keeping traffic moving smoothly	22	49	15	6	7
detecting and arresting people involved in violent crime	21	45	14	4	16
patrolling the streets in police cars	20	49	18	7	6
dealing with rowdy, loutish and drunken behaviour	19	47	16	5	12
working with groups in the community	14	39	19	7	21
providing help and support to victims of crime	13	36	17	6	28
dealing with white-collar crime	10	36	15	6	31
detecting and arresting burglars	8	35	28	14	14
patrolling the streets on foot	8	25	29	32	7

Weighted data, half core sample. Unweighted case count ranges from 5039 to 5059 cases. Responses are ranked by the per cent responding "very good."

Patrolling on foot and by car

Two questions were about police patrolling. Patrolling was one of the jobs that members of the public felt informed about. Few (6-7 per cent) said they did not know how good a job the police did at patrolling. But opinions were mixed about police effectiveness.

Twenty-five per cent of those interviewed thought the police did a fairly poor or very poor job of patrolling the streets in police cars, and 61 per cent of respondents were dissatisfied with foot patrol. In general, big-city residents and people who were worried about crime or who felt their neighbourhoods were deteriorating were more likely to be dissatisfied with police patrolling performance, as were victims of crime.

At the same time, residents of inner and outer London were more satisfied than the rest of England and Wales with police patrolling. The 1992 BCS sample was large enough to examine them separately in many instances, and revealed that residents of inner London were particularly positive about police foot patrol; 17 per cent thought police did a very good job at this, as contrasted to seven per cent of people living outside London. Residents of inner and outer London were also more satisfied than others with patrolling by car.

There was a strong correlation between how satisfied respondents said they were with patrolling by the police and with those respondents remembering having seen an officer recently on the beat. Almost 20 per cent of the people interviewed recalled having seen an officer on foot in their area in the past week. Those respondents were much more likely to think highly of police foot patrol. Police visibility levels explained a great deal of the satisfaction of London residents. In inner London, 49 per cent of the people interviewed recalled having seen an officer on the beat in the past week. In outer London, the figure was 27 per cent.

In the BCS set of 13 questions on aspects of police work, respondents who were dissatisfied with foot or car patrol were more likely to be generally dissatisfied with police performance than were respondents dissatisfied with other police tasks. Research generally finds that the public expects a higher level of patrolling by car and especially on foot than it receives, and the dissatisfaction that this generates is clear.

Fighting crime

There was also some dissatisfaction, and more self–confessed ignorance, with the police's crime-fighting abilities. Responses to questions about burglary, violent crime and white-collar crime are included in this cluster. Three of the bottom four rankings in Table 2.1 refer to police effectiveness in controlling crime. The public was evenly split between whether or not they thought the police did a good or poor job at detecting and arresting burglars; 43 per cent thought they did, and 42 per cent thought they did not.

This division is significant because surveys of the public find that the public ranks burglary as one of the most serious crimes. A Harris survey placed burglary just slightly below sexual assault on the public's agenda for police time and energy, and the people surveyed also rated burglary as one of the most common problems in their community (Joint Consultative Committee, 1990). Burglary is an area of police responsibility in which public confidence has been falling. In several surveys, Gallup (1992) has asked people how much confidence they had in the ability of the police "...to solve minor crimes like burglaries...". In 1983, 47 per cent of people said they had very great or considerable confidence in this but, by 1992, that figure had dropped to 32 per cent.

On the other hand, only 18 per cent of people interviewed felt the police did not do a good job at detecting and arresting violent criminals. This ranking accords with differences in police clear-up rates for violent crime and burglary, which in 1991 were 77 per cent and 27 per cent, respectively. Public confidence in the way the police tackle violent crime has remained high over the years. In 1983, 67 per cent of the public had very great or considerable confidence in the police's ability "...to solve major crimes, like bank robberies...". In 1992 that figure was only slightly lower at 64 per cent (Gallup, 1992).

Forty-six per cent of those interviewed thought the police did a good job at dealing with white-collar crime, but 31 per cent of those questioned admitted they did not know anything about this aspect of police work. Forty-nine per cent thought the police did a good job at providing help and support to crime victims, but 28 per cent did not have an opinion about this.

Women, the elderly and people on low incomes were more likely to think the police did a good job at dealing with crime. Interestingly, responses in this cluster were not particularly related to fear or worry about crime. Residents in big cities, victims of crime and respondents who had had some contact with the police were more negative. Residents of inner London were the least satisfied with the police's handling of both burglary and violent crime. About a quarter thought the police did a very poor job with burglary cases, and 12 per cent felt likewise about the police's handling of violent crimes; the comparable figures for the rest of England and Wales were 15 and 5 per cent, respectively. Victims were particularly likely to think that the police did not do a good job at giving help and support to victims. Afro–Caribbeans were also more negative in their ratings of police effectiveness against violent crime and burglary.

Regulating traffic

Public assessments of police work in regulating traffic were very positive. Seventy-six per cent of the people interviewed thought the police did a good job in dealing with serious motoring offences, and 71 per cent felt the police made a good job of keeping traffic moving smoothly. Like routine patrolling, traffic control is a visible police activity, and most respondents felt they were informed about it. Residents of inner London were less positive than others about the ability of the police to keep traffic moving smoothly.

Women, lower-income and older people were most likely to feel the police were effective at controlling traffic. But such people were also less likely to drive a great deal and be exposed to traffic enforcement. Respondents who had been stopped recently by the police were somewhat more likely than others to think that the police did a poor job. Another group with a negative view of police traffic enforcement was heavier drinkers. In the 1992 BCS, respondents were asked to characterise their level of alcohol intake, on a scale ranging from "never" to "drink heavily". Almost 70 per cent described themselves as light-to-moderate drinkers or abstainers. Those near the heavy-intake end of the scale were more likely to think police did a poor job at regulating traffic, as well as at most other police tasks.

Another highly rated police activity was responding to accidents and medical emergencies. Ninety per cent of people interviewed thought the police did a good job at this. People living outside London were more satisfied with this aspect of police performance.

Relations with the community

Two questions gauged the public perception of how well the police related to the community. Sixty-seven per cent of the people questioned thought the police did a good job at giving the public advice on how to prevent crime, and only 11 per cent had no opinion on this increasingly important matter. Slightly more than 20 per cent did not have an opinion about how good a job the police did in working with groups in the community; among those with an opinion, twice as many thought the police did a good job as thought they did a poor job.

Older people and home owners thought police did a good job, as did respondents who personally knew an officer. Victims of crimes against their person or their property, residents of big cities and respondents who perceived high levels of physical decay and social disorder in their area were among those who did not think the police did a good job at relating to the community. Residents of inner London were less likely than those living elsewhere to be satisfied with the police's work in crime prevention or in the community.

Controlling disorder

BCS respondents had a generally positive view of the performance of the police in controlling disorderly conduct. Almost 80 per cent thought the police did a very good or fairly good job at controlling crowds at sporting and public events, and two-thirds approved of how the police dealt with rowdy, loutish and drunken behaviour. The view that the police did a good job at controlling crowds and public drinking was more common among older and more educated people. Respondents who had been arrested themselves did not share this opinion; nor did those who had been stopped on the street by the police in the past year. Not surprisingly, self–reported heavier drinkers also took a less sanguine view of such police efforts. When asked how good a job the police did at dealing with loutish and drunken behaviour, 31 per cent of self-reported abstainers thought the police did a very good job, compared to only 15 per cent of people who said they drank "quite a lot".

A general index of opinion

As well as considering these clusters of responses separately, it also proved useful to combine them into one general index of opinion of the police service. This index will be used in the next chapter to examine the impact of people's experiences of the police on public opinion. (For a discussion of the index, see Appendix A.) A multivariate analysis of the correlates of this index confirmed the independent strength of many of the factors described earlier.

Sex and age were the strongest demographic correlates of opinion, with women and older people giving police performance higher ratings. Recalling having seen the police patrolling on foot was even more influential; ratings of performance were substantially higher among those who had recently seen police on the beat. But this influence on opinion was confined to whites and Asians. The police-performance ratings given by Afro-Caribbeans were not related to police visibility.

That link was also weaker in younger men than in older men or women of all ages. Knowing a police officer (" ...well enough to talk to by name") was also independently related to people being more satisfied with the performance of the police. On the other hand, recent victims, people who had contacted the police about some matter and heavy drinkers were less satisfied. There was also more dissatisfaction with the police shown by people living in disorderly neighbourhoods.

Living in inner or outer London was not significant once other features of people's lives were taken into account, but public satisfaction with patrolling by the police and dissatisfaction with traffic control by the police in London were significant.

A final factor related to how people felt about the performance of the police was the mass media. To assess its effect, respondents were asked how they got most of their information about the behaviour of the police. Most people (64 per cent) said that television, radio or newspapers were their most important sources of information on the behaviour of the police. Another 11 per cent judged that most of what they knew came from their own experiences of the police; and 17 per cent said they got their information by talking to people they knew. Five per cent did not know where they got their information about the police.

Taking into account all the other variables discussed here, people who got most of their information about the police from the media were more positive than others in their assessments of policing. The media seemed to cast a positive light on the performance of the police, while respondents who had had recent direct experience of the police were more negative.

Conclusions

Earlier sweeps of the BCS documented a decline in satisfaction with police performance, and, in particular, a sharp drop in the number of people who thought their local police did a very good job. There was evidence that this decline was widespread and that it included groups that previously were quite supportive of the police. To monitor this trend, the Home Office sponsored several more surveys, and the 1992 BCS included a special supplement of questions about the police.

As a whole, these surveys show that the level of public confidence in the police fell a little between 1988 and 1992, but that the dramatic decline in the number of people giving the police their highest vote of confidence has stopped. The 1992 BCS also shows some recovery in victims' satisfaction with the handling of their cases by the police.

The BCS also documents much variation in how the public viewed police effectiveness in various tasks. The police were thought to do a particularly good job at dealing with crowds, traffic and accidents. Their perceived effectiveness at dealing with burglary, white-collar crime and crime victims came near the bottom of the list, along with patrolling on foot.

Generally, women and older people thought the police did a good job; residents of disorderly and crime-ridden neighbourhoods did not. Police visibility (measured by a question about the police patrolling on foot) and personal acquaintance with an officer were related to higher levels of public satisfaction with police performance. Many people did not know enough about the police to give them a rating for some of the questions, especially the questions about controlling crime.

Across the board, respondents with more direct experience of crime and the police were more likely to have opinions, but their opinions were more negative than the views held by respondents with less personal experience. The influence of the mass media seemed to have led people to rate the police more positively.

3 Contact with the police

The experiences people have of the police are an important determinant of public opinion. Chapter 2 reported that assessments of how well the police did their job were generally lower among people who had recently had contact with them. Not surprisingly, those who had been stopped by police were more negative, and people who had repeatedly been stopped were even more so. People who had contacted the police were more negative than people with no direct experience of the police; and the more contact people had had with police, the more negative their views became.

This chapter examines the nature of people's experiences of the police to discover why this might be so. It describes who contacted the police, why they did so, how the police responded, and the impact of people's experiences on their assessments of the quality of police service. The patterns this chapter uncovers are complex because the public engages the police in a number of roles: as clients needing help, as customers of services being offered by the police, as targets of police enforcement efforts, and as voters and tax payers. Almost everyone relates to the police in one of those categories, and many in several of them.

Frequency of contacts

To examine the frequency of their encounters with police, BCS respondents were presented with a checklist of 17 typical circumstances in which they might have contacted the police in the previous year. These circumstances ranged from reporting a crime in which they had been the victim to asking for directions or the time. Respondents were also asked how often each form of contact had occurred during the year, and which encounter was the most recent. Detailed questions were then asked about the most recent contact, which was the one most likely to be fresh in their minds. They were also asked if they had been stopped by the police while in a car or on a motorcycle, or while on foot. Detailed questions were also asked about these encounters.

It should be remembered that these questions were asked of half the sample, so some figures in this and following chapters will differ a little from those in Mayhew *et al.*, whose figures were based on all the crime victims in the 1992 BCS.

Fifty-four per cent of those interviewed recalled an encounter with the police in the previous year. A few more people contacted the police than were approached by them, but many people had some recent experience to recount. Tables 3.1 and 3.2 detail the frequency of these contacts. Table 3.1 describes contacts that were initiated by the public. This table combines responses to the detailed questions into five general categories. (Appendix Table B.2 presents figures for each of the original 17 questions.) About 16 per cent of those interviewed recalled contacting the police about a crime; this

Table 3.1
Frequency of Citizen-Initiated Contacts With The Police

Type of Contact (One or More Times)	Per cent
To report a crime against oneself, a household member, or anyone else	16
To report a car or burglar alarm; a suspicious person or circumstance; a disturbance, noise or nuisance; or another problem or difficulty	14
To report a traffic accident or medical emergency; a missing person; something lost or found; that a home would be empty; or other sorts of information	14
To ask for directions, the time, advice, or information	6
For a social chat	2
Total: contact initiated by the public	39

Weighted data, half core sample. Total sums to more than percentages because of multiple overlapping

Table 3.2
Frequency of Police-Initiated Contacts With The Public

Type of Contact (One or More Times)	Per cent
Approached or stopped while in a car or on a motorcycle, as a driver or passenger	16
Contacted by police to return missing property or an animal; to deal with a ringing burglar alarm; to ask for information about a crime; or another reason	14
Told or asked to contact the police, in order to show documents or give a statement	4
Contacted by police to investigate a noise or disturbance; to investigate an accident or offence respondents were involved in, or to search their homes or make an arrest; to ask them to move on	4
Stopped and asked questions while on foot	3
Total: contact initiated by the police	31

Weighted data, half core sample. Total sums to more than percentages because of multiple overlapping was the most frequent form of contact initiated by the public. About three-quarters of these contacts were about crimes in which respondents or members of their households had been involved, and about one-quarter were about crimes that had involved other people. In their report on the 1992 BCS results, Mayhew *et al.* (1993) also deal with respondents who reported crimes to the police, but their analysis is restricted to respondents who reported offences that they themselves or members of their households had experienced.

The next most frequent form of contact (14 per cent of respondents) was to give the police information. People's most common motive was to inform the police of accidents, but they also called to let the police know that something had been lost or found, or that their home would be empty. The same proportion of people contacted the police to report some kind of disturbance, including ringing alarms, suspicious persons or circumstances, and noises or nuisances. Another six per cent of the people interviewed recalled contacting the police to ask for advice, directions, the time or other information. Finally, about two per cent recalled contacting an officer "just for a social chat".

In all, 39 per cent of those interviewed recalled making contact with the police at least once during the previous year; 30 per cent had made contact once, and 9 per cent more than once. One respondent insisted that he had contacted the police 60 times, but the most frequent category was one contact, and 98.5 per cent of all respondents recalled initiating fewer than 10 contacts with the police during the year.

The frequency of many of the contacts does not appear to have changed substantially from the figures in the 1988 BCS. Because of changes in the questioning sequence, the two surveys are not directly comparable; the 1988 survey focused on how respondents contacted the police (via 999, etc.), but the 1992 questionnaire focused on why people had contacted the police. In the 1988 survey, about 13 per cent of respondents recalled reporting a crime; in 1992, the comparable figure was 16 per cent. In 1988, 12 per cent of respondents contacted the police to give them information; in 1992, it was 14 per cent. And, in 1988, about nine per cent reported some kind of disturbance, compared to 14 per cent in the most recent survey.

Encounters initiated by the police

Table 3.2 summarises who often respondents recalled having been stopped by the police, the police having come to their house, or having been required to go to a police station. In this report, these are all classified as police–initiated encounters, and they were also quite common. The most frequent police–initiated encounters were when respondents had been stopped in a car or on a motorcycle. This applied to 16 per cent of the people interviewed, and about one-third of those recalled having been stopped more than once.

About 14 per cent of the people interviewed had been contacted by officers who were dealing with ringing alarms, asking for information about crime, or returning recovered property. Another three per cent of people had been stopped and asked questions by police while they were on foot; in this report, these encounters are dubbed "pedestrian stops". Four per cent had found themselves compelled to show documents or give a statement at a police station.

The final category of police–initiated encounters includes those in which respondents had themselves been the subject of suspicion and had been contacted in the course of an investigation. This category also includes respondents who had been involved in an accident or an offence, had been making a disturbance, whose homes had been searched, or who had been arrested. Respondents who reported having been " asked to move on" were also classified in this group, which included 4 per cent of all adults.

Like public–initiated encounters, these contacts overlapped. In all, about 31 per cent of BCS respondents had been involved in a police–initiated contact during the year. There was a significant increase over 1988 in the percentage of respondents who recalled having been stopped while in a vehicle, from 12 to 16 per cent. On the other hand, the 1992 figure of three per cent for pedestrian stops was identical to that in the 1982 and 1988 sweeps. In 1988, seven per cent reported having had to report with documents or for questioning at a police station, which is quite close to the four per cent figure for 1992. Trends for London matched those in the rest of England and Wales; pedestrian stops stayed constant at three per cent, but the percentage of respondents who reported having been stopped in motor vehicles increased from 11 per cent in the 1988 survey to 17 per cent in 1992.

Contacts initiated by the public

Who contacted the police?

Better–off, more educated people were more likely to contact the police. BCS respondents with household incomes of more than £20,000 a year were more likely to contact the police for every reason, including to report a crime. Overall, 50 per cent of people in this income range reported having contacted the police during the previous year, but only 31 per cent of those earning under £10,000 a year had done so. This difference persists when the effects of a number of other social and economic factors related to contacting the police are taken into account by using multivariate logistic regression analysis. This procedure isolates the independent effect of each factor (in this case income), and takes into account how the factors are related to one another, as well as to the dependent variable (here a dichotomous measure of whether or not each BCS respondent recalled initiating a contact with the police during the year).

Home owners were somewhat more likely than council-housing dwellers to have contacted the police. London residents, and inner-city residents elsewhere, were also more likely than others to have contacted the police, especially about crime.

Afro–Caribbeans and Asians were less likely than whites to have contacted the police, except to report a crime; in that category, there were no differences among the races. Men had had more contacts than women, as had people living in households with children and those having access to cars or motorcycles. There was also a substantial difference in the rate at which unemployed people had contacted the police about a crime; they were also more likely than others to recall having often contacted the police. Victims of crimes were only slightly more likely to contact the police for any reason, except to report a crime. These patterns closely resemble those described in Smith's (1983) study of Londoners and the 1988 BCS. Table B.3 in Appendix B presents detailed tabulations of contact patterns.

What happened?

The 1992 BCS draws a brief portrait of these encounters, one that enables us to probe some of the sources of the satisfaction or dissatisfaction felt by people who had contacted the police. People recalling contact were asked detailed questions about their most recent encounter, because those incidents were most likely to be fresh in their minds. They were asked about the speed with which the police had arrived, and about the effort the police had made and the interest they had shown in the case. These factors are all thought to affect people's perceptions of the quality of the police service (Ekblom & Heal, 1982). Table 3.3 divides encounters into the categories that were outlined earlier, including contacts about crime, disturbances, and the giving or receiving of information. (The experiences of the 107 respondents recalling social chats are excluded here.)

Respondents were asked first if they had had any face-to-face contact with the police about the matter, a factor that in the 1988 BCS was related to satisfaction with the police service. If they had not, they were asked if, in their view, the police should have seen them or someone in their household about the matter. Not surprisingly, face-to-face contacts were common after a crime had been reported and less frequent after respondents had reported a problem or had given the police information. Despite the high rate of face-to-face contact to follow up the reporting of crime, 26 per cent of people who had not been contacted thought they should have been. That also applied to 15 per cent of those who reported disturbances or other problems, and to 13 per cent of those seeking information.

There was less room for complaint about the speed at which police responded. In every category, almost 80 per cent or more of people who had contacted the police said that they had not had to wait for them to respond, or that they had waited only a reasonable

Table 3.3
What Happened During Citizen-Initiated Contacts

Description of Contact	About Crime	Suspicion, Alarms and Disturbances	To Give Information	Ask For Information
	%	%	%	%
Met with the police face-to-face	71	50	58	68
(IF NO) Did not meet but should have with someone	26	15	0	13
No wait or a reasonable wait before the police attended to the matter	79	78	82	88
Police showed as much interest as they should	70	78	83	88
Gave the matter as much effort as they should	65	72	85	85
Kept respondent very or fairly well informed	26	24	35	43
(IF NO) did not keep informed but should have	45	31	25	24
How polite in dealing with respondent				
fairly or very impolite	3	5	7	0
fairly polite	25	25	19	28
very polite	72	69	74	72
Range of unweighted cases for questions asked of all respondents	163-174	140-173	149-173	42-50

Weighted data, half core sample. Social chats are excluded.

length of time. In every category, at least 95 per cent of people who had contacted the police thought they had been treated very politely or fairly politely.

The survey also asked how much effort respondents felt the police had put into dealing with their case, and about how much interest the police had shown. The 1988 BCS found that these were significant sources of public dissatisfaction with policing. In 1992, about one-third of those reporting a crime thought police had given the matter less effort than they thought it had deserved, and about 30 per cent thought the police had not shown appropriate interest in what they had to say. People who had reported disturbances and suspicious circumstances were more satisfied with police efforts, and public satisfaction with various forms of information sharing was even higher.

The BCS shows that the largest gap between public expectations and police performance stemmed from the feeling that officers had not kept people informed about their case. As Table 3.3 documents, only 26 per cent of those respondents who had reported crimes – and substantially fewer than a majority in any category of encounter – thought they had been kept very well or even fairly well informed. Many people felt they should have been kept better informed. This was particularly true of those respondents who had contacted the police about a crime; 45 per cent of those people who felt they had not been kept informed thought they should have been.

The BCS shows that different categories of people using the police service received somewhat different levels of service. People reporting crime expressed the most discontent, followed by people complaining about disturbances, suspicious circumstances and alarms. A subset of those reporting a crime, victims themselves, were even more disgruntled. They were significantly less likely than non-victims to think they had been kept informed, that the police had made enough of an effort in their case or (less strongly) that the police had even been interested in what they had had to say.

The kind of service that people felt they had received was also related to their social background. Compared to whites, Asians and Afro-Caribbeans were more dissatisfied in several ways. Both minority groups were about twice as likely as whites to report that they had had to wait an unreasonable length of time before the police had attended to their complaint. Seventy-seven per cent of whites thought the police had taken appropriate interest in their case and 75 per cent thought the police had put enough effort into their case; among Asians and Afro-Caribbeans, those percentages were in the low 60s. Seventy-three per cent of whites reported that the police had been very polite, but only 65 per cent of Afro-Caribbeans and 44 per cent of Asians thought so.

Age was also related to perceptions of the quality of service provided by the police. Younger people who had contacted the police were much less likely to report that their complaint had been given enough effort or that police had been interested in what they had had to say, and they were less likely to think they had been treated politely. In general, residents of metropolitan and inner-city areas reported slower police response times, and that the police had shown less interest and effort than they thought desirable. But inner-London residents were particularly likely to say they had been treated politely and had been kept well informed.

Satisfaction with the police service

In addition to specific questions about what had happened during each encounter, the BCS included two questions assessing general impressions of the event. Respondents were asked how satisfied or dissatisfied they were with the way the police had handled the matter, and if their experience made them more or less favourable to the police in general. The results are presented in Table 3.4

The largest reservoir of dissatisfaction was among those who had contacted the police about a crime; about one-third of them were dissatisfied with how their case had been handled. About one-quarter of respondents were unhappy about how their calls about alarms or disturbances had been handled. People who had given or asked for information from the police were much more satisfied with the service they had received. It is interesting that, on the whole, people who had contacted the police did not think that their opinions of the police had changed very much. By a slight margin, people who had contacted the police about a crime were more likely to report that they had changed their mind. The number of people whose views had been affected were evenly balanced between those who had become more favourable and those who had become more unfavourable in their attitudes to the police.

Table 3.4
Satisfaction With Citizen-Initiated Contacts

Description of Contact	About Crime	Suspicion, Alarms and Disturbances	To Give Information	Ask For Information
	%	%	%	%
Overall satisfaction with the way police handled the matter				
very dissatisfied	15	12	5	8
a bit dissatisfied	17	10	8	4
fairly satisfied	35	33	35	26
very satisfied	31	40	52	63
How favourable did the contact make respondent feel about the police in general				
less favourable	13	9	5	6
no difference	75	82	87	85
more favourable	12	9	8	10
Range of unweighted cases for questions asked of all respondents	163-174	140-173	149-173	42-50

Weighted data, half core sample.

Respondents' answers to the questions about their satisfaction with the way a matter was handled by the police and about how favourable that experience made them feel towards the police in general were statistically related to descriptions of what happened when respondents called the police. This allowed us to probe which aspects of police performance had the most effect on popular satisfaction with policing. It also enabled us to isolate the independent effect of each of the aspects of the police service described in Table 3.4, and to judge their relative importance. In both instances, four factors stood out:

* keeping people informed about what was happening;
* acting politely;
* exerting the effort that seemed called for;
* showing enough interest in what they had to say.

The precise ranking of these four factors varied a little between the two measures of public satisfaction, but the statistical impact of these four factors was considerable. The importance that the public attributes to being kept informed has been documented in research on crime victims, for whom this is a leading complaint (Shapland and Vagg, 1987; Burrows, 1986). Fifty per cent of BCS respondents who had contacted the police about a crime and who felt they had not been kept informed were dissatisfied. But only six per cent of respondents who felt they had been kept very well or fairly well informed felt dissatisfied. (Appendix Table B-4 presents a detailed breakdown of respondents' dissatisfaction by the various events that occurred during respondents' encounters with the police.)

The 1988 BCS found the belief that the police had not really been interested in people's problems was the second leading reason for dissatisfaction with police performance. That factor was also important in the 1992 BCS findings. Almost three-quarters of those who felt the police had not been as interested as they should have been in the reported crime were either very or fairly dissatisfied, as opposed to only 15 per cent of those who felt the police had shown appropriate interest. "Not doing enough" was the most frequent complaint in 1988. In the 1992 BCS, perceived lack of effort is also a powerful predictor of public satisfaction with the police service. Seventy-four per cent of respondents who had reported a crime and who thought the police had not shown enough interest were dissatisfied, as contrasted to 13 per cent of those who were pleased with the level of police effort.

Perceived response time was linked to satisfaction. Respondents who thought that the police had not responded quickly enough said they were dissatisfied and that they felt less favourably towards the police as a result. However, few respondents felt that they had had to wait too long for the police to come.

On the other hand, almost 30 per cent of people who telephoned the police about a crime – and 50 per cent in the disturbance-and-suspicion category – had not had face-to-face contact with the police. Lack of face-to-face contact with the police had a negative effect on other public assessments of police performance, including the effort and interest people felt had been shown by police in the case and whether callers felt they had been kept informed. In turn, these factors moulded people's overall judgements of the service they had received. Face-to-face contact was particularly salient for those respondents who had been victims of crime (see Mayhew *et al.*, 1993). This point is of some significance because the number of crime-related calls leading to face-to-face contact with the police declined by about 10 percentage points between 1988 and 1992.

Satisfaction with the quality of police service in these situations was also linked to people's social background. Afro–Caribbeans and Asians were less likely to think the police had been interested in their case or had given it enough effort, and were also more likely to think the police had responded slowly and had not kept them well-enough informed. Asians were most likely to feel they had not been treated very politely. Younger respondents, the unemployed and council-housing residents also followed this pattern. Inner-London residents were among the most satisfied, but in other inner-city and metropolitan areas satisfaction was lower.

To people who had contacted the police, what mattered was how they had been treated. Most of the links between people's social background and general assessments of the police service are explained by the variations in why people had contacted police and how they had been treated when they had contacted the police. This is illustrated in Figure 3.1. The statistical analysis on which this is based used rsponses to the general measure of service quality described in Chapter 2, which assesses perceived quality of service across multiple activities.

Younger respondents were somewhat more negative in their views than their experience would predict, but otherwise the factors sketched in Figure 3.1 summarise the apparent dynamic of public-initiated encounters with the police. Social background and the problems people bring to the attention of the police played an important role in determining the character of the police response. What happened in the field in turn shaped people's overall assessment of the quality of police service.

Experience seems to be the only link between social background and judgements made about the quality of policing, which suggests that measures to improve the police service could have a great impact on consumers' views of the service. The data are consistent with the expectation that, for example, new measures to keep people who contact the police informed about the case could reap significant benefits. The efforts the police put into solving problems may also not come to the attention of the people who initially reported those problems. Finding ways to bring the efforts of the police to the notice of the public would also keep the public informed. Finally, refocusing officers' attention on displaying their concern, and their professional efficiency, might pay dividends in public support.

Figure 3.1
Service satisfaction

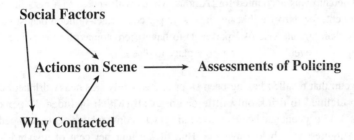

Contacts initiated by the police

Table 3.2 documents the frequency of various police-initiated contacts with the public in the 1992 BCS. People were most often stopped in cars or on motorcycles. Sixteen per cent of BCS respondents had been stopped in this way by the police. Three per cent of the people interviewed had also been stopped while on foot. Four per cent had been contacted by police investigating an offence, had had their homes searched, or had otherwise been the subject of police investigations. Those groups overlapped considerably; for example, 30 per cent of people who had been stopped as pedestrians had also been involved in motoring incidents. In total, 22 per cent had been stopped or investigated by the police in one way or another (these incidents will all be referred to as " stops" below).

Another 14 per cent of those interviewed had been visited by police to render some service, such as to return missing property or deal with a ringing alarm. These encounters are dealt with separately, because they involve very different police-public dynamics.

Who was stopped by the police?

Encounters instigated by the police were sharply delineated along socio-economic lines. Such encounters were more likely to involve men, those under 25 years of age, single and unemployed people, and Afro-Caribbeans. Appendix Table B.3 details these patterns. Men were almost twice as likely as women to be stopped. Thirty-six per cent of Afro-Caribbeans, and 46 per cent of all respondents under 20 years of age, recalled having been stopped by the police. These groups were also more likely to recall having been stopped several times in the course of the year.

Fifteen per cent of Afro-Caribbeans recalled three or more stops, but the figure for the population as a whole was just 3 per cent. Council-housing dwellers and low–income people were less likely than the more affluent to report having been stopped, partly because they owned fewer cars. Almost one-quarter of car or motor cycle owners had been stopped, but only 11 per cent of people living in households without one.

On the other hand, racial differences in traffic stops were even more exaggerated when vehicle ownership was accounted for. Among whites with access to a car, the stop rate was 18 per cent; for Afro-Caribbeans, it was 42 per cent. Inner-London pedestrians were more likely than anyone else (4.2 per cent) to have been stopped by the police. Motor-vehicle stops were evenly distributed from place to place.

Another group that recalled having been stopped frequently was heavy drinkers. Among those who claimed to drink only little or not at all (which included 37 per cent of respondents), 13 per cent had been involved in vehicle stops and two per cent in pedestrian stops; both figures were below average. But, of the four per cent of respondents who characterised their alcohol intake as heavy, or said that they drank quite a bit, 29 per cent recalled having been involved in a traffic stop and 12 per cent in a foot stop; eight per cent recalled three or more stops, also above average.

When the respondent's self-confessed alcohol intake was included with other factors in a multivariate logistic regresssion analysis, self-confessed heavy drinkers continued to stand out as having been targets of police stops. Other groups that had been disproportionately involved in police-initiated stops were males, youths, single people and those with cars.

What happened?

The 1992 BCS asked detailed follow-up questions about traffic and pedestrian stops, two of the most frequent ways in which police initiated encounters with the public. The responses to these questions paint a fairly detailed portrait of respondents' views of what transpired during those incidents. As in encounters initiated by the public, what happened during these police-initiated encounters related to people's assessments of how they had been treated by the police.

As described in Table 3.5, about half of those stopped thought they had been stopped because police believed an offence of some sort had occurred. A slim majority of pedestrian stops occurred in people's own neighbourhoods, but most vehicle stops took place elsewhere. Those who had been stopped on foot were typically alone at the time; drivers frequently had had one or two passengers with them. Officers gave reasons for making almost all traffic stops, and for three-quarters of pedestrian stops. These usually were interpreted as "good reasons" by the people involved, especially if they were driving at the time.

Table 3.5
What Happened During Police-Initiated Contacts

Description of Contacts	Vehicle Stops	Pedestrian Stops
	%	%
Was this because the police thought an offence had been committed?		
thought offence committed	51	43
stop for some other reason	49	57
Location of the encounter?		
own neighbourhood	38	57
somewhere else	62	43
How many others 16 years or older were with the respondent?		
no others	38	55
1-2 others	51	23
3 or more others	11	22
Did the officer give a reason for stopping you?		
no	8	22
yes	92	78
(IF YES) Would you say this was a good reason (for stopping you)?		
no	18	18
yes	82	82
Were respondent, others or vehicle searched?		
no	93	78
yes	7	22
(IF YES) Did the officer fill out an official form about the search?		
no	69	79
yes	31	21
Were respondent or others involved prosecuted?		
no	93	97
yes	7	3
Was someone arrested, breath-tested, issued a vehicle or fixed penalty notice, told to take documents to a police station, have their name and address taken, searched, or prosecuted		
no	62	74
yes	38	26
Range of unweighted cases for questions asked of all respondents	743-751	131-132

Weighted data, half core sample.

Few of those involved in traffic stops (seven per cent) had been searched, but 22 per cent of pedestrians who had been stopped were searched by the police. These figures do not differ significantly from 1988, when 10 per cent of traffic stops and 22 per cent of pedestrian stops included searches[1]. In both cases, less than one-third of those searched recalled the officer filling out an official report of the incident, as is usually required by the Police and Criminal Evidence Act.

Respondents were also asked how fairly and politely they had been treated when stopped, and if the police had taken enough interest in what they had had to say. These views are summarised in Table 3.6. It is apparent that outright inpoliteness was quite rare during these encounters, and that the bulk of respondents felt they had been treated quite fairly or even very fairly. A significant number of those involved in car stops (34 per cent) felt that police had not taken enough interest in what they had had to say, perhaps reflecting the routine nature of many traffic infringements.

About 40 per cent of people caught up in traffic stops had then been sanctioned, as had one-quarter of people in foot stops. The term sanction in used broadly here, and includes arrests, breath tests, vehicle-defect or fixed-penalty notices, mandatory reporting to a police station, being searched or prosecuted, or having one's name and address taken by an officer.

As Table 3-5 shows, few of those interviewed reported that they had been prosecuted. Seven per cent of those involved in traffic stops said that they had been prosecuted as a result. The figure for 1988 was 10 per cent, which is not significantly different. About four per cent of those involved in pedestrian stops had been prosecuted; the 1988 figure was three per cent.

Especially in the case of pedestrian encounters, these data point to a great deal of low-visibility, highly discretionary policing. Many respondents had been stopped and questioned without any formal action having resulted from it. Whether or not something had happened as a result was related to the social background of those involved. Among those who had been stopped either on foot or while driving, youths, males, unattached individuals, low-income respondents, council-housing residents and racial minorities were sanctioned more often.

How people were treated during these encounters was related to the circumstances under which they had been stopped and to who they were. As Table 3.5 shows, traffic encounters seemed to have been conducted more routinely than pedestrian stops. Drivers were more likely to have been given what they considered good reasons for the stop. Drivers were less likely to be searched and more often a form had been filled out by the

---

[1] In 1982, 13 per cent of those involved in traffic stops reported having been searched. The decline in this figure to 7 percent in 1992 is statistically significant.

Table 3.6
Evaluation of Most Recent Police-Initiated Contact

Assessments of Contact	Vehicle Stops	Pedestrian Stops
	%	%
How much police interest in what you had to say?		
as much as should	59	70
less than should	34	25
don't know	7	4
How polite were they in dealing with you?		
very polite	55	45
fairly polite	31	32
fairly impolite	8	15
very impolite	5	7
don't know	1	0
How fairly would you say the police treated you?		
very fairly	56	43
quite fairly	32	35
quite unfairly	7	15
very unfairly	4	7
don't know	2	0
Range of unweighted cases for questions asked of all respondents	739-752	129-132

Weighted data, half core sample. Excludes 22 offence-related contacts classed as " other" incidents.

officer responsible. As Table 3.6 shows, drivers were also more likely to perceive they had been treated politely and fairly.

It is likely that pedestrians are stopped under more ambiguous circumstances and because of less readily acknowledged infringements of the law. Some effects of this can be seen in Tables 3.5 and 3.6. People had more often been stopped on foot for reasons that they thought had been unrelated to an offence. The police had been more circumspect about their intentions (they had less often given reasons for having made the stop), and they had made more searches. At the same time, the police had also listened more often to what people had had to say, and had less often ended up arresting or otherwise sanctioning someone. But, perhaps inevitably, these stops had seemed more unfair.

Afro-Caribbeans and Asians were more likely than whites to be searched if they were on foot, but race was not related to searches following traffic stops. In both circumstances, racial minorities were more likely to feel they had been treated unfairly and impolitely, and that the police had not taken enough interest in what they had had to say.

When describing pedestrian stops, younger respondents were more likely to report that officers had not given them reasons for stopping them, and that, when the police had done so, those reasons had not been good ones. Younger respondents were also more likely on all occasions to have been searched and sanctioned in some fashion. Like racial minorities, they also thought they had been treated unfairly and impolitely, and that the police had not taken enough interest in what they had had to say.

Higher-income respondents involved in traffic stops were more likely to have been given what they thought were good reasons for having been stopped. Higher-income respondents were less likely than others to have been searched or sanctioned in any way. They also reported that they had been treated more politely and fairly. When contrasted to council residents, home owners' experiences closely paralleled the experiences of respondents with higher incomes.

Women recalled having been more considerately treated across the board. Women were more likely to remember having been given what they considered a good reason for having been stopped, especially if they had been on foot at the time. Women had been searched less often, and more often a form had been filled out if they had been searched. They had been sanctioned more rarely, and they more often perceived that they had been treated fairly and politely, both in pedestrian and traffic stops.

Table 3.7

Satisfaction With Most Recent Police-Initiated Contact

Satisfaction With Contact	Vehicle Stops	Pedestrian Stops
	%	%
Overall satisfaction with how police handled the matter?		
very satisfied	48	38
fairly satisfied	33	29
bit dissatisfied	10	14
very dissatisfied	8	19
don't know	2	1
Did this contact make you feel... ?		
more favourable	12	9
no difference	76	70
less favourable	11	20
don't know	1	0
Range of unweighted cases for questions asked of all respondents	739-752	129-132

Weighted data, half core sample. Excludes 22 offence-related contacts classed as " other" incidents.

Satisfaction with encounters

The reactions of people who had been stopped by the police were assessed by follow-up questions asking how satisfied they were with how police had handled the matter, and if the encounter had led them to be more or less favourable towards the police. The results are presented in Table 3.7. The largest reservoir of dissatisfaction with police-initiated encounters was concentrated in those who had been stopped on foot. One-third of those stopped while on foot were dissatisfied to some degree with how police had handled the matter. In general, respondents judged that their experience had not had an effect on their general impression of the police. For traffic stops, those whose views had changed split about evenly in terms of whether they become more or less positive, but the split was much more negative among those stopped as pedestrians.

Not surprisingly, what happened during these encounters played a substantial role in shaping opinion. Across the board, respondents who had been searched or sanctioned were unhappy about it, as were those who had not been given reasons for having been stopped. For example, only 13 per cent of pedestrians who had not been given a reason for having been stopped were very satisfied with the experience, but 45 per cent of those who had been given a reason felt that way. The strongest determinants of how satisfied they felt were indicators of the manner in which the police conducted themselves. Roughly in the order given below, the strongest correlates of satisfaction were:

* treating people fairly;
* acting politely;
* showing enough interest in what people had to say.

For example, if officers were perceived as having paid attention to what people had had to say, 61 per cent of respondents stopped in vehicles were very satisfied with how the encounter had been conducted; of the rest, only 24 per cent were very satisfied.

The events that transpired during these stops, and the manner in which officers conducted themselves, almost totally account for the link between public assessments of the quality of the police service and social and economic divisions in the population. At first examination, such factors as age, race, sex, income, marital status, and even self-reported drinking habits were strongly linked to satisfaction with policing, as measured by the general index described in Chapter 2. But almost all of those linkages were channelled through people's experiences. Taking into account perceived fairness, politeness, interest, and such factors as whether or not respondents had been searched or given reasons for having been stopped, accounted for most of the variation in opinion. An important exception to this was race: taking into account these factors, Afro-Caribbeans were still more negative about policing than one would predict.

Otherwise, how the police had conducted themselves at the scene played the most powerful role in shaping public opinion. As above, this suggests that efforts to improve specific aspects of police behaviour could have significant advantages. The most important of the factors examined here were perceived politeness and fairness, and the extent to which respondents had been given reasons for having been stopped. These were both strong predictors of popular satisfaction and there was some scope for improvement in these aspects of police behaviour, especially during pedestrian encounters.

Complaints against the police

Anyone who believes that the police have acted improperly can make a formal complaint. Detailed procedures for the handling of such complaints are prescribed by the Police and Criminal Evidence Act 1984. These procedures require chief police officers to record and investigate complaints against members of their force. Depending on the seriousness of the complaint, the police may attempt to allay the grievance by an informal resolution procedure (a formal complaint is, nevertheless, recorded).

In other cases, or if informal resolution fails, the complaint will be fully investigated and a report made to the Police Complaints Authority (PCA), a body independent of the police. The PCA scrutinises the chief officer's decision whether to take any disciplinary action and writes to the complainant about the outcome of the investigation. The PCA may also supervise the investigation of more serious complaints. In cases where a criminal offence may have been committed, the Director of Public Prosecutions decides whether criminal proceedings should be instituted.

The 1988 BCS found that most complainants who had made formal complaints against the police were concerned about police demeanour. The most frequent complaints were that the police had been overbearing, rude, arrogant or unfriendly in their dealings with the public; that the police had made unjustified accusations; that they had used undue force; that they had been incompetent, had not adequately investigated a case or had failed to take appropriate action.

The 1992 BCS also questioned respondents about whether they had been annoyed enough about a police officer's behaviour, either towards them or someone they knew, to feel like making an official complaint. Because of the rarity of official complaints, respondents were asked about events over the past five years. The survey found that 21 per cent of respondents recalled having been "really annoyed" at an officer during that period. The reasons they had been annoyed (or, if they had been annoyed on more than one occasion, the most recent reason) are summarsed in Table 3.8. One third had been concerned about aspects of police performance (summarised at the bottom of Table 3.8), and 71 per cent with the personal behaviour of the police (summarised at the top of Table 3.8).

Table 3.8
Annoyance and Complaints About Police

Nature of Annoyance	Per cent of Persons who were annoyed	Per cent of Persons who Complained
Poor Demeanour	71	67
rude, arrogant, unfriendly, over-casual	40	38
behaved unreasonably, unfairly	39	46
used undue force, assaulted someone	8	21
racist language or behaviour	2	3
Bad Performance	35	47
inaction; didn't do enough	16	15
incompetent or inappropriate action	9	15
behaved illegally; broke the rules	6	16
slow response; police did not come	5	7
poor follow-up; did not keep informed or come back	6	6
offender not caught; property not recovered	2	–
Other reasons	6	4
Number of respondents	1028	98
Number of complaints	1445	157

Weighted data, half core sample. Note that respondents could be annoyed more than one way, so the percentages sum to more than 100 per cent. Percentages for the major categories account for overlaps in complaints within their subcategories. "–" indicates less than 1 per cent.

The leading concern about on-the-job performance was the perception that the police had not done enough, or had done nothing at all, about some matter. Appearing to be incompetent was also a frequent problem. Forty per cent of those who had been annoyed had been concerned about police who had been rude, arrogant, unfriendly, or had adopted what was interpreted as an over-casual manner. Almost an equal number of people believed the police had behaved unreasonably or unfairly on some occasion in the past. Very few people had been concerned about the use of excessive force or racist remarks.

Respondents who had had direct experience of the police were most likely to have had a problem. People who had contacted the police, who had been stopped by the police, or who had been crime victims, had the most to say. Self-confessed heavy drinkers, Afro-Caribbeans and younger respondents also were more likely to recall having been annoyed. All of these groups were also more likely to have felt like making their complaint a formal one.

Of the 21 per cent who had been annoyed about some matter, 45 per cent (or 10 per cent of the total sample) had felt like making an official complaint about it. But, of those who had been predisposed to file a complaint, 81 per cent had not. About three per cent said that they had tried to file a complaint but had not succeeded, and 16 per cent (about two per cent of the total sample) had actually made a formal complaint. Table 3.8 summarises their concerns, which closely resemble the overall distribution of annoying circumstances.

The few who had made a complaint (or had tried to, but failed) had not been very satisfied with how their case had been handled by the police. Almost 70 per cent had been very dissatisfied or fairly dissatisfied with what had happened. Young people, Asians and Afro-Caribbeans were in that group; older and more affluent complainants had been more satisfied.

A comparison of these figures with those from the 1988 BCS shows that there was a great deal of consistency in public opinion of police behaviour. In 1992, 21 per cent of those interviewed recalled an annoying circumstance; in 1988, it was 20 per cent. In both surveys, almost an identical percentage had felt like making a complaint, and the percentage of them who had actually filed a complaint was 16 per cent in 1992 and 20 per cent in 1988.

Changes in survey procedures make it difficult to compare all the reasons that people had to be concerned about the police, but in comparable categories there were no significant changes between 1988 and 1992. In 1988, 36 per cent of those who had been annoyed had been concerned about rude, unfriendly or arrogant behaviour; in 1992, it was 40 per cent. Police inaction had been a concern of 16 per cent in 1988 and 15 per cent in 1992; racist behaviour had been a problem for one per cent in 1988, and two per cent in 1992. None of these differences is statistically significant.

Conclusions

This chapter has examined encounters between the public and the police. It detailed who had been stopped by the police and who had contacted them, why these encounters had taken place, and what the police had done. These factors were related to one another. Basic features of people's lives shaped their need for police assistance, and also affected their risk of being stopped. Who people were, and why they had been stopped, were also linked to what the police had done at the scene.

In all, it is estimated that 54 per cent of adults in England and Wales had some encounter with the police during the course of the year. About 30 per cent of those interviewed had contacted police about some matter, 22 per cent had been stopped or investigated in some way, and 14 per cent had been visited by officers rendering some service. The most notable difference between these figures and those for 1988 was the frequency of traffic stops, which rose from 12 to 16 per cent. The rate at which police had stopped people on foot was identical to that in 1988, and there was no significant change in the likelihood that the police would search someone once stopped. The most frequent kind of public-initiated encounter is to report a crime, and that also had not increased significantly between 1988 and 1992.

Higher-income people and residents of larger metropolitan and inner-city areas were more likely than others to have contacted the police; racial minorities were less likely. Like the 1988 BCS, this survey illustrated the frequent dissatisfaction of crime victims and those contacting the police to report a crime. These are the people who rely most on the police, and who are seen by many as one of the core constituencies that the police serve. However "the less urgent the matter, the more satisfied the public" (Jones *et al.*, 1986).

About one-third of those who had contacted the police about a crime felt the police had not shown enough interest or given the case enough attention, and only about one-quarter felt they had been kept well enough informed. Another group, those calling to report suspicious circumstances, disturbances, ringing alarms and nuisances, had also often been dissatisfied with how their complaint had been handled, and for the same reasons. These people are the police's eyes and ears. Such people are being encouraged by Neighbourhood Watch and other schemes to make those calls more frequently, but almost a quarter of them are coming away dissatisfied with how their calls are handled.

As in past studies, the 1992 BCS also registers high levels of dissatisfaction among racial minorities and younger people, both with how they are treated when stopped by police and with how their cases are handled when they call on the police for information, advice or help. They were less likely than others to have thought that their problems had received enough attention or effort, or that they had been kept well enough informed. Repeated surveys by Gallup find the same concentration of dissatisfaction in those reporting crimes and disturbances, and the same pattern of reasons for this dissatisfaction (Southgate and Crisp, 1992).

Police-initiated encounters, such as pedestrian or traffic stops and other investigations, were more likely to involve young men, single and unemployed people, heavy drinkers and Afro-Caribbeans. In only 38 per cent of vehicle stops and 26 per cent of foot stops had people been given good reasons why they had been stopped and sanctioned in some way. Most people involved in traffic stops thought they had been treated fairly, but that the police had not shown much interest in what they had had to say.

The police had shown more interest in what people stopped on foot had had to say (as much as they had shown to respondents reporting a crime), but more than one in five of these people thought they had been treated very unfairly or quite unfairly. People stopped on foot were treated less politely than those who had initiated police contact. But, compared to those respondents who had called the police about a crime, more of the people involved in foot stops declared themselves very satisfied or fairly satisfied with how the police had handled the matter.

It is also important to note what people had not been dissatisfied with, or what had not seemed to affect their overall judgments about policing. Most of the people contacting the police (80 per cent or more, depending on the problem) had been satisfied with the time it had taken the police to respond. Those who thought the police might have come faster were not particularly dissatisfied with how their case as a whole had been handled, or with policing generally, once other sources of their disgruntlement had been accounted for. Even among those who had been annoyed by the police, only five per cent had been annoyed by the time the police had taken to respond.

Almost no one complained about offenders not having been caught or property not having been recovered, which could be considered the, so to speak, bottom line of policing. Most public-initiated contacts had been handled courteously, as had 80 per cent or more of police-initiated contacts. In every category, at least 95 per cent of people contacting the police thought they had been treated very politely or fairly politely. When the police had stopped respondents, they had given, by and large, what people considered good reasons for doing so. Overtly racist language or behaviour had also not come to the surface very often, according to people's recollections of what had annoyed them.

The BCS helps explain how the public's experiences of the police were translated into opinions of the quality of policing in England and Wales. These opinions were assessed by a general index based on responses to 13 questions rating various aspects of police performance. General assessments of policing by respondents with recent experience of the police, such as having been stopped or investigated, or having had occasion to contact them during the previous year, were related to how their case had been handled and how they had been treated.

A polite demeanour and paying attention to what people had had to say for themselves paid off for policing, both in police-initiated and public-initiated encounters. Acting in what was perceived to be a fair manner had positive results in police-initiated contacts with the public; making a visible effort and keeping callers informed paid dividends in public-initiated calls on the service of the police.

This suggests that new measures to keep people who contact the police informed about their case could reap great benefits, as could focusing more public attention on the efforts that police put into solving problems and finding ways to keep the public informed of what action the police are taking. Officers need to display comforting concern as well as an aura of professional efficiency. For those who had been stopped by police, the most important factors shaping their opinion were politeness and fairness, and the extent to which respondents had been given reasons for having been stopped. These were strong predictors of satisfaction and there was some scope for improvement in them, especially during pedestrian encounters.

Of course, all of these conclusions are based on perceptions and judgements gathered from the perspective of people who received some service from the police or who were the focus of police attention. There are limits to the reliability and completeness of such perceptions and judgements (see McConville and Shepherd, 1992). Some respondents would have misjudged or have been ignorant of what the police were doing on their behalf. Officers handling their cases may have had good reasons for doing what turned out to be unpopular, or actions that they took may have remained hidden from public view.

In many circumstances, more aggressive efforts by the police to communicate their good intentions and good works might have led to their appearing in a slightly better light in the survey. Such efforts might be dismissed as mere marketing, but the Quality of Service Programme is strongly committed to improving how the delivery of the service is viewed by consumers. The 1992 BCS shows that exchanging information more freely with the public would enhance rather than undermine support for the police.

Likewise, this and other research suggests that communicating expectations about what the police can realistically accomplish might overcome the view of some people that the police are not doing enough. As long as public expectations are set by the media they may be unrealistically high, and thus easily dashed by reality. Instead, the police may wish to engage in educating the public about what the police can be expected to do and what they should be held responsible for. The police should acknowledge their mistakes, refute unfair criticism, and be justly proud when they do a good job.

On the other hand, BCS respondents would also have interpreted their experiences at least partly in the light of attitudes that they had already formed, and in some sections of the population those attitudes are not very favourable. This presents a more difficult problem for the police, but the 1992 BCS suggests that recent, direct, favourable experiences of the police play a very important role in shaping general opinions. Among those respondents who had been stopped or had contacted the police themselves, what they had then experienced was powerfully related to what they thought about policing generally. Pockets of alienation may subside according to the extent that patterned differences in the delivery of police services can be smoothed out.

HOME OFFICE RESEARCH STUDY No. 134

4 Reporting crimes to the police

Introduction

One purpose of crime surveys is to examine unreported offences. Surveys of crime victims around the world have revealed that what is known as the "dark figure" of unreported offences is substantial and accounts for half or more of some categories of crime (Skogan, 1984). This chapter describes the factors related to the reporting of crime. It is guided by past research on the topic, which suggests that reporting is determined by the seriousness of the crimes.

Past research also suggests that a host of factors, ranging from victims blaming themselves to the quality of police service they expected to receive, also affect the likelihood that crimes will be brought to the attention of the police. What happened once the police were notified of a crime has been examined in Chapter 3, as well as in another report on the 1992 BCS by Mayhew *et al.* (1993).

Decisions by eyewitnesses, victims and their family members or confidants to report crimes have many implications for the community and the legal system. The effect of these decisions is great because perhaps as much as 75 to 85 per cent of crimes discovered and reported by victims and witnesses (Joint Consultative Committee, 1990). Private insurance and public compensation for crime victims depend on these people making formal reports. Almost all victim-support schemes rely heavily on the police to identify and refer victims in need to these schemes, and those whose experiences go unreported may be cut off from assistance and support.

Patterns of reporting and non-reporting play an important role in setting the priorities of the police, who are largely a reactive force. Non-reporting protects selected classes of perpetrators, including those who abuse relatives and family members who are reluctant to involve the police. Police resources may be misallocated if crime reporting varies a great deal from place to place, or if selected offences are systematically shielded from official view. By shielding offenders from official attention, non-reporting limits the capacity of the criminal justice system to deter.

On the other hand, those reporting differences that are related to social factors, such as the perpetrator's race, could distort the apparent distribution of offending and the profile of what seems to be the typical criminal entering the criminal justice system (see Shah and Pease, 1992). Non-reporting certainly threatens the validity of official crime rates, if we do not know the extent to which crime rates rise and fall in response to changes in reporting rather than in response to the rate of crime itself. It is for this reason that surveys of crime victims are often used to evaluate crime-reduction programmes that might affect the willingness of victims to step forward or the process by which the police make official records of crime.

Crime reporting in the BCS

The BCS presents a 10-year picture of crime-reporting rates in England and Wales. The reporting trend has fluctuated from survey to survey, but the rate is definitely up. The proportion of all offences that victims said had come to the police's attention rose from 31 per cent in the 1982 BCS to 43 per cent in the 1992 BCS. Reporting of household burglary rose from 66 per cent in the 1982 BCS (and 63 per cent in the 1988 survey) to 73 per cent in the 1992 survey; the reporting of successful burglaries (those with a loss) went from 85 to 92 per cent.

Reporting of vandalism is up significantly, and there has been a large increase in the reporting of thefts of personal and household items. The reporting of vehicle thefts also rose significantly, from 95 per cent in the 1982 survey to 99 per cent in the 1992 BCS. Reporting of the subset of BCS offences that are defined in the same terms as police statistics went up very significantly between 1982 and 1992, from 36 to 50 per cent, and this accounts partly for the increase in officially recorded crime over that period. (For a discussion of trends in reporting and the implications of those trends, see Mayhew & Aye Maung, 1992; Mayhew et al., 1993.)

How does the BCS measure crime reporting? In the survey, respondents are first asked if they have experienced any of a long list of crime incidents during the previous calendar year. They are then asked a series of detailed questions about each offence that they recalled, including (near the end of the questions) whether or not the police came to know about the incident. If respondents thought that the police had not known about the matter, respondents were asked why not. If respondents said that the police had been informed, they were asked a series of questions about how the police had come to know about the crime and what the police had done in response.

There are several important points to note in this approach. Those who were selected for interviewing were sometimes not in a good position to say much about the reporting process. In 42 per cent of all incidents someone else, not the respondent, had reported the incident; this was most frequently the case for assaults and thefts. As a result, respondents could sometimes not answer further questions about the police response. Victims of multiple offences sometimes had too much to tell interviewers, so, to simplify matters, detailed questions were asked about only the first three incidents respondents recalled.

Many details were also skipped if the crime had occurred outside England or Wales. In addition, because the BCS is a survey of households, it does not fully represent all recorded crime. It excludes crimes against organisations and commercial establishments, and it cannot account for the many crimes that the police learn about and clear up by questioning suspects and informants.

Also, about six per cent of those questioned who thought the police had not known about the incident said that they had reported it to some other authority, such as a company security officer or their supervisor at work. This confounds any statistical profile that treats these respondents as non-reporters, and the survey cannot reveal what the recipients did with those complaints.

Crime reporting in the 1992 BCS

Like past surveys, the 1992 BCS documents that most crimes involving individuals and households are not reported to the police. Table 4.1 presents reporting rates for major categories of crime.[1] As it shows, only about a quarter of assaults and less than a third of household thefts or vandalism were reported, and less than half of all property thefts and robberies or thefts from the person. The only categories in which more than half of the offences were reported were burglary, thefts of or from cars and bicycle theft.

An examination (not shown) of more detailed categories of crime establishes an even wider range of reporting. At the top, 99 per cent of car thefts were reported, and 93 per cent of the small number of arson attacks uncovered by the survey. At the other end of the spectrum, only 8 per cent of attempted thefts from the person were reported.

Almost exactly two-thirds of these incidents were reported by telephoning a local police station, rather than by dialling 999 (11 per cent), personally visiting a station (19 per cent), or approaching an officer on the street (2 per cent). Assaults were most often dealt with by 999 calls (although fewer than a majority of incidents were reported in that way). Victims of robbery and theft from the person most frequently made a personal visit to a police station.

Reporting by telephone was most common when crimes occurred at home; 999, in particular, was employed when victims were attacked or threatened, when weapons or serious injuries were involved, for job-related incidents, and when relatives, neighbours or friends were identified as the offender. Asian victims were distinctively likely to use 999 as well. Victims tended to visit a police station when the crime occurred away from home, when it was a property offence, and when they did not know much about the identity of the offender.

---

[1] Eleven incidents in which the victim was a police officer are included in Table 4.1, but excluded elsewhere in this chapter.

Table 4.1
Crime Reporting in the 1992 BCS

Type of Crime	Per cent Reported	Average Seriousness	Unweighted Cases
Vandalism	27	4.3	1020
vehicles	25	4.4	625
households	31	4.1	397
Burglary	73	8.2	678
attempts and no loss	53	7.0	328
burglary with loss	92	9.3	350
Theft of motor vehicles	99	8.7	255
Theft from motor vehicles	53	5.2	1049
Attempted theft of or from vehicles	41	5.4	431
Bicycle theft	69	5.4	261
Other household thefts	29	3.8	766
Wounding	48	9.3	101
Robbery and theft from person	38	6.8	166
Other personal thefts	38	4.7	382
Common assault	26	6.3	280
All offences	43	5.6	5392

Core sample weighted data for up to three incidents per respondent occurring in England or Wales.
Number of cases is for crime reporting.

What accounts for the wide range of crime reporting documented here? Past research has isolated a number of relevant factors. Many of them reflect aspects of the seriousness of the crime, and those factors also play an important role in this report. But more than the seriousness of a crime is involved. The 1992 BCS asked victims to rate how serious they thought their experience had been. They were instructed to use a 0-20 scale. Zero was exemplified as the theft of a milk bottle from the doorstep; 20 was exemplified as murder. The average seriousness ratings for major offence categories are also given in Table 4.1, where it can be seen that such ratings cannot always be translated into reporting rates.

Bicycle theft was rated with the same seriousness as attempted theft of or from cars, but was reported almost 70 per cent more frequently. Woundings and successful burglaries were ranked with the same seriousness, but their reporting rates were 48 and 92 per cent, respectively. Car theft was rated twice as seriously as vandalism to cars, but was reported four times more often.

Among more detailed categories (not shown), the small number of sexual offences uncovered in the survey were given a high seriousness rating (an average score of 11 in the 0-20 scale), but had a low reporting rate (18 per cent). Robbery and threats were given almost identical seriousness scores, but the reporting of them differed by 10 percentage points. Clearly, other features of crimes, victims and offenders also play a role in reporting.

Data on factors that might explain these differences in reporting were collected in the 1992 BCS. It reveals that crime reporting in England and Wales by and large reflects processes that are at work around the world. The discussion that follows reviews the major factors that were linked to reporting in the BCS, and then uses multivariate statistical techniques to isolate the effects of the most important of these factors. This was necessary because the experiences people had had of crime were interrelated with one another, and with other important aspects of their lives. The following discussion begins with relationships between victims and offenders, because these relationships permeated almost every aspect of crime reporting.

Victim-Offender Relationships

The BCS documents the long-standing supposition that crimes among those who know and, perhaps, love one another are less likely to be brought to the attention of the police. One of the most troubling aspects of domestic violence is the extent of the desire to shield the offence from view. Incidents that involve victims and offenders who live together or nearby, or who are related or somehow close friends, can reflect complex relationships that the parties may prefer to keep behind closed doors.

In this analysis, what is called a "related-party" case includes family members, current or former marital or cohabiting partners, or household members. The category of what is called "well-known" offenders includes workmates, clients, neighbours, acquaintances, children from the community, and others that victims said they knew well. Crimes in both categories were less likely to be reported than those involving casual acquaintances or strangers.

In the BCS, when respondents said that crimes had not been brought to the attention of the police, respondents were asked why not. The reason that it had been a private, personal or family matter was given by 55 per cent of victims of related-party crimes;

overall, this reason was given for 14 per cent of unreported personal crimes and one per cent of property offences.[2]

On the other hand, not knowing much about who had committed the crime was also a reason for not reporting crimes to the police. Feeling unable to shed much light on who had committed the crime can discourage victims from reporting the crime to the police, especially when victims do not feel compelled by other factors. Twenty-seven per cent of respondents who had been the victims of strangers volunteered the reason for not reporting the crime as "the police could have done nothing". Only 10 per cent of those who had been the victims of parties who were well known to them offered this explanation.

The most basic fact about offenders is that, in a large majority of all offences, victims do not have the slightest idea who did it. The BCS probed first for a demographic description of offenders. Then victims were asked if they had known any of them, and how well they had known them. About 77 per cent of property crime victims would not hazard a guess even about how many offenders had been involved. Only 19 per cent knew if the perpetrators had been men or women, and more than 90 per cent of all property offences are classified in this report as crimes by strangers.

In only three per cent of property crimes had offenders been well known to victims or somehow more intimately related. Not surprisingly, victims of personal crimes could often identify offenders by their numbers, genders, and apparent races; 92 per cent of respondents said that they could say something about the perpetrator, and 91 per cent recalled the sex of their assailant. But crime victims often knew little about the perpetrators' identities. Victims described offenders as complete strangers in 44 per cent of cases, and in an additional 14 per cent of incidents had just seen them around.

On the other hand, about 15 per cent of victims identified offenders as related to them, or as current or former marital partners or household members; 14 per cent described their assailants as workmates, clients, neighbours or acquaintances. These two categories, plus some of the remaining 12 per cent of offenders described by victims as someone they had just spoken to casually, encompass the pool of offenders that could be most readily identified to the police, if those offences were reported to them. But these offences often go unreported.

Table 4.2 describes the relationship between crime reporting and the ability of victims to say something about offenders. The results are divided between personal and property crimes.Among victims of property crimes, there was a clear distinction between stranger and non-stranger crimes, with the latter being reported at a higher rate.

---

[2] Personal crimes include assaults, sexual offences, robbery and snatch thefts and threats of personal violence. Property crimes include burglary, all other personal and household property thefts and criminal damage. The categories include attempted and accomplished crimes that fell within the range of incidents counted by the BCS.

This accords with victims saying they had not reported a crime because they had had little information to give the police. But the link between victim-offender relationships and crime reporting is reversed in the case of personal crime.

Among victims of personal crimes, reporting was associated with *not* knowing offenders, or recognising them only by sight or just having spoken with them casually. Reporting rates dropped when victims knew their attackers well or were even more intimately linked to them. This effectively shielded three-quarters of those offences

Table 4.2
Relationships, Intrusiveness and Reporting to Police

Per cent Known To The Police	All Crimes	Personal Crimes	Property Crimes	All Crimes Unweighted Cases
Could the respondent say anything about who did it?				
no	43	28	43	4257
yes	41	32	55	1753
Victim-offender relation:				
stranger/unknown/don't know	44	32	46	5213
seen or know by sight	39	35	46	300
know or speak to casually	38	37	32	172
know well	36	28	52	186
relative or partner	29	25	56	139
Incident location				
home/garage	59	31	68	1027
near home	38	43	38	2822
at/near work	41	31	48	1358
elsewhere	38	28	48	1358
Was the crime job related?				
no	42	30	46	5161
yes	43	39	48	368
Did the offender have a right to be at the location?				
no	58	55	59	967
yes	39	30	43	5024
Total Unweighted Cases	6012	856	5156	6012

from the view of the police. So, the few property crimes in which victims had thorough knowledge of the offenders were more likely to be reported than to be shielded from view; the reverse was true for victims of personal crime.

Victim-offender relationships are further entangled with other aspects of crime. For example, victims of intimate offences are more likely to need a doctor and to visit a hospital, and upper-income people are more often the victims of strangers. Both of these factors are also associated with a higher level of reporting, so their effects will be examined in a multivariate analysis later in this chapter. In addition, these sample data probably under-estimated the aggregate impact of close victim-offender relationships on the extent of officially recorded crime.

An important limitation of victim research is the often documented weakness of surveys at assessing the extent of related-party crimes: methodological studies show that such crimes are less likely to be mentioned in survey interviews than crimes committed by strangers. As a result, BCS estimates of the frequency of related-party crimes are likely to be below the true total, and the overall impact of intimate relationships on the extent of officially recognised domestic and related-party crime is likely to be even greater than suggested here.

Seriousness of the threat

The BCS also measured a number of factors that provide an index to the seriousness of crimes. One set of indicators points to how potentially threatening incidents were, either because they put life and limb at risk or because they intruded into the sphere of privacy that many people assume surrounds them while they are at home. Table 4.2 illustrates differences in reporting that were associated with the intrusiveness of crime. Intrusiveness is indicated by the location where each incident occurred and by whether or not the offender had a right to be there when the crime took place.[3] Both were linked to crime reporting. Incidents at home (mainly burglaries) stand out in the case of property crime; 68 per cent were reported to the police. Property crimes committed by offenders who had the right to be where they were also proved less likely to be reported.

The reporting of personal crimes did not follow the same pattern; offenders who had a right to be at the scene were again shielded from the view of the law, but crimes committed at home were not more likely to be reported. Multivariate analyses show that this was because of the close association of personal crimes at home with offenders whom victims had known well and had, therefore, been less likely to report to the police.

---

[3] Offenders were scored as having a right to be at the scene if the crime had taken place out of doors, on public transport, while the victim had been shopping or if the crime had been perpetrated by someone the victim had come into contact with while working. If the crime had taken place inside somewhere, offenders who had been, for example, guests or workmen were scored as having a right to be at the scene where the crime had taken place.

In the multivariate analysis to be presented below, all of these factors prove to have great effect on the likelihood of crimes being reported.

Another venue vulnerable to intrusion is the workplace, Job-related personal crimes were more likely than others to be reported by nine percentage points. As noted above, reporting to people other than the police is another option in many workplaces. Overall, 20 per cent of incidents that were not apparently brought to the attention of the police had been reported to some other authority. The most common job-related incidents were personal thefts, and almost 40 per cent of those had been reported to someone other than the police.

Measures in Table 4.3 describe the extent to which crimes threatened victims' personal safety. The small number of personal thefts in the property-crime column in which some threat had been made were much more likely to be reported. But this was not true of other personal crimes. Reporting rates were almost identical in forceful or threatening circumstances and non-forceful or non-threatening categories. How could this be? What turns out to be a straightforward and expected link – that crimes involving force and threats of force are more likely to be reported by victims – was again masked by the effects of assaults by non-strangers, which were very numerous and went unreported for different reasons.

The use of a weapon also raises the stakes in crime, and the seriousness of the threat caused by this should encourage crime reporting. Fortunately, firearms were not often used in the crimes described in the BCS. Use, or threatened use, of some other kind of weapon was described in about 16 per cent of personal crimes; these included bottles, screwdrivers, clubs and knives. As Table 4.3 shows, such crimes were not reported that frequently. But three-quarters of the very few crimes involving a gun (they numbered only 10) had been reported to the police.

Seriousness of injury and loss

Another important factor determining how likely a crime is to be reported is the degree of harm inflicted on victims. The harm suffered by victims may be financial, physical or emotional, and measures of all of those dimensions were strongly related to the frequency of reporting in the BCS.

Two financial consequences of crime are depicted in Table 4.3 These are the value of property stolen and the extent of any property damage inflicted on victims and their households. Respondents' financial losses have been grouped into categories for presentation in Table 4.3, but more precise estimates of these losses were gathered in the survey. The value of stolen or damaged property was related to the reporting of both personal and property crime, and reporting was high when losses of more than £200 were incurred.

On the other hand, cases where there had been little damage to property, and when the goods stolen were valued at less than £50, were reported as infrequently as crimes incurring no financial loss. Theft and damage tended to occur together (the correlation between the two losses was +.26), but in multivariate analyses both were highly significant predictors of crime reporting.

Table 4.3
Threat, Injury, Loss and Reporting to Police

Per cent Known To The Police	All Crimes	Personal Crimes	Property Crimes	All Crimes Unweighted Cases
Threat to safety				
no force or threat	44	44	45	5345
threatened (only)	34	34	79	239
force used	na	32	na	428
Weapon involvement				
no weapon; don't know	42	31	46	5790
other type of weapon	36	33	60	163
firearm	na	75	na	10
Value of property stolen				
none	33	30	35	2933
£ 1-49	25	39	24	966
£ 50-199	56	55	56	869
£ 200 plus	90	75	90	912
Value of property damaged				
none	36	31	39	3404
£ 1-49	38	30	38	752
£ 50-199	62	69	61	718
£ 200 plus	81	-	81	472
Was there an insured property loss?				
no theft, loss or insurance	32	31	34	3457
insured loss	60	69	60	2555
Total unweighted cases	6012	856	5156	6012

Core sample weighted data for up to three incidents per respondent occurring in England or Wales. Don't know responses excluded unless noted. "-" indicates less than 10 sample cases. "na" indicates not applicable.

Wanting to recover lost property or to make a claim on private <u>insurance</u> provides an additional reason for contacting the police. In the US National Crime Survey, thefts of insured property are more than twice as likely to be reported as losses of uninsured property, and the difference between insured and uninsured burglary thefts is almost as great. Pease (1988) found that insurance accounted for many of what were described as "anomalous" reportings of low-seriousness property crimes in the 1984 BCS.

In the 1992 BCS, victims were asked if any of their stolen or damaged property had been covered by an insurance policy. As Table 4.3 illustrates, crimes with an insured property loss were almost twice as likely to be reported as crimes with uninsured property losses. All of these financial factors proved to be important even when several other determinants of reporting were controlled for; for example, we shall see in a later section that an insured loss drives reporting up by almost eight per cent.

There was also a strong link between the <u>emotional impact</u> of crime and how likely it was to be reported. Victims were asked if they or anyone in their household had had any emotional reaction to the crime, and follow-up questions gathered information on how the crime specifically affected family members. Overall, someone was described as having been upset in 72 per cent of incidents.

The most common emotional response was anger, which was reported by almost all victims. Anger was followed by shock (33 per cent of all reactions) and fear (22 per cent of reactions). Of all those who had had an emotional response, 44 per cent were described as having been very much affected. People had been upset by having been victims of every type, although slightly less often by criminal damage to property.

As reported in Table 4.4, the emotional impact of having been a victim was strongly linked to reporting of property crimes; half the crimes that had an emotional impact had been reported, as contrasted with 36 per cent of those that had not had this effect. Victims of reported crimes were more likely to experience shock and difficulty sleeping, as well as anger.

In the personal-crime category, there was not a straight–forward link between emotional impact and the reporting of crime; reporting rates were almost identical in affected and unaffected victims. This was because victims had been more upset when they had had an intimate association with the perpetrator and when the crime had taken place at home, both factors that otherwise were associated with lower levels of crime reporting. But, when those factors are controlled for, offences with emotional consequences have about a five per cent greater chance of being reported to the police.

A final measure of the extent of harm to victims is offered by responses to questions about the <u>physical harm</u> caused by crimes. Non-fatal injuries were fairly common, either the respondent or someone else had been reported injured in 52 per cent of personal crimes. Some of those injuries apparently were quite minor, because only 21 per cent of those incidents (and 11 per cent of all personal crimes) had needed a doctor's attention. The most frequently reported were black eyes and bruises, which made up 54 per cent of all injuries. Cuts and broken bones made up 29 per cent of injuries, and scratches 13 per cent.

Table 4.4 describes the relationship between injury and the reporting of personal crimes. In this report, injury cases are defined as crimes causing bruises, scratches, cuts, broken bones or black eyes, plus all rapes and sexual assaults. Injuries that also needed the attention of a doctor or a stay in hospital are classified separately in Table 4.4 Using whether or not the attention of a doctor had been needed as a means of identifying the most serious injuries proved to be important. Injuries that had not needed a doctor were less likely to be reported to the police than incidents that had not involved any injury at all.

Table 4.4
Crime Impact and Reporting to Police

Per cent Known To The Police	All Crimes	Personal Crimes	Property Crimes	All Crimes Unweighted Cases
Was anyone injured?				
no injury	na	31	na	5559
injury-no doctor	na	24	na	305
injury-doctor	na	62	na	142
Did a household member have an emotional reaction?				
no	35	32	36	1673
yes	44	31	50	4335
Was any household member responsible in some way for what happened?				
no	43	34	46	5146
yes	36	22	42	859
Total unweighted cases	6012	856	5156	6012

Core sample weighted data for up to three incidents per respondent occurring in England or Wales. "Don't know" responses excluded. "na" indicates not applicable.

Why should this be? Again, much of the puzzle is linked to other factors that shape the reporting of crime. In this case, it is partly because of the strong tie between personal violence causing injury and the relationship between the parties. In the BCS, 80 per cent of all personal crimes involving people related to one another had led to an injury, and one-third of those injuries had called for the attention of a doctor. Sixty per cent of personal crimes in which victim and offender had known each other well had led to an injury.

On the other hand, 60 per cent of crimes committed by a stranger had led to no injury at all. Torn between the consequences of injury and the ties of close relationships, victims who had been injured short of needing a doctor's attention had apparently been swayed by the desire to shield the incident from public view. Injuries were also more common among young, low-income and unemployed people with a history of having been victims in the past, and these groups had generally been less willing to step forward when they had been victims of crime.

Culpability

Past research suggests that the behaviour and identity of victims play a role in their decision to report crimes to the police. The 1984 BCS showed that self-confessed offending was quite widespread, ranging from 41 per cent in those who had the opportunity steal office supplies from their place of work to three per cent of all adults smoking cannabis (Mayhew and Elliott, 1990). Using sketchier self-report data from the 1982 BCS, Maxfield (1988) found that a third of personal-crime victims in London had themselves been the targets of pedestrian or traffic stops by the police in the same year. In addition, victims may be loath to report trouble they get themselves into. In the first American victim survey, 25 per cent of victims agreed that they had done something foolish or negligent to contribute to their plight. In a London survey, Sparks, Genn and Dodd (1977) included questions probing the frequency of illegal acts by those being interviewed. They found that victims who were also self-reported offenders were less likely than others to report to the police that they had been victims of crime

The 1992 BCS asked if the respondent, a household member, or someone else had been responsible in any way for what had happened, because of something they had done or had forgotten to do. About 16 per cent said someone had been responsible in some way, and, as shown in Table 4.4, this group was significantly less likely to report offences to the police. Respondents who admitted some culpability were evenly divided between those who had suffered personal and property offences. Culpability was most common in bicycle-theft victims; 37 per cent admitted that they had contributed to their plight. Other high-culpability offences were woundings and common assaults; simple household and personal thefts; and crimes in which offenders were well known, related, neighbours or friends.

Other culpability factors, such as whether victims had been drinking at the time of the offence or if they had begun a fight in which they had eventually been the loser, were not assessed by the 1992 BCS. Self-confessed heavy drinking was not linked to crime reporting, but victims who had been stopped by the police while on foot were significantly less likely than others to report personal and property offences. It appeared that victims had been worried about how they might have been labelled by the police, and that this, coupled with shame or embarrassment, played some role in their reporting of crime.

Socio-economic Factors

Table 4.5 shows that the likelihood of reporting crimes was low among less affluent victims, and rose steadily with increases in total household income, especially when the crime was personal. Both of these patterns were statistically significant but, when other factors are controlled for (see below), the direct effect of income on crime reporting disappears. This is because household income is linked to several factors that have positive effects on crime reporting.

In particular, higher-income households had lost more cash and goods of higher value, and had suffered more property damage in the course of their having been victims of crime. They were also much more likely to be insured. High-income victims were less likely to describe an intimate link with an offender, a factor that inhibits victims from reporting offences.

Higher-income people were also less likely to have previously been victims of crime, which is also a factor linked to lower reporting levels. There is also a strong and persistent link between home ownership and crime reporting, and that factor also seems to account for some of the apparent link between income and the reporting of crime.

Unlike some other countries, the effects of race and age on crime reporting are not strong in England and Wales. Table 4.5 describes low reporting rates for personal crime by youths but, unlike the US and Holland, these differences disppear when other factors are taken into account. As in surveys in other countries, older victims are more likely than most to report crimes to the police, but that pattern is not apparent in the BCS until other factors are controlled for; when they are, people over 60 are about four per cent more likely to report crime.

Racial differences in crime reporting are complex. As shown in Table 4.5, Asians were most likely to report personal crimes, but there were few differences between the races in the reporting of property crimes (this analysis used a special booster sample of ethnic minorities, so it is based on a substantial number of interviews). But the kinds of crimes that various groups are caught up in differ substantially. Black Americans report crime at

Table 4.5
Culpability, Social Background and Reporting to Police

Per cent Known To The Police	All Crimes	Personal Crimes	Property Crimes	All Crimes Unweighted Cases
Victim 1-4 years ago of burglary, personal theft, assault or sexual assault				
no	45	40	46	4408
yes	35	24	44	1604
Race* white	42	32	46	5631
Afro-Caribbean	41	35	43	747
Asian	46	42	48	648
Age 16-19	25	15	41	412
20-29	43	36	46	1520
30-39	44	34	47	1507
40-49	47	45	47	1147
50-59	47	41	44	653
60 and older	44	41	45	758
Housing Tenure*				
home owner	43	33	46	4024
council	38	32	41	1269
private rental	42	27	52	674
Household income				
£0-2,499	31	17	42	521
£2,500-9,999	38	30	42	1708
£10,000-19,999	45	37	47	1633
£20,000 or more	47	42	49	1696
Is there access to a telephone?				
no	40	31	45	786
yes	42	32	46	5216
Total unweighted cases	6012	856	5156	6012

Core sample weighted data for up to three incidents per respondent occurring in England or Wales. 'Don't know' responses excluded. Data by race includes booster sample. *indicates small "other" categories are excluded from this table.

least as frequently as whites because the crimes that they recalled in the US National Crime Survey tended to be more serious than those described by whites.

A similar pattern, albeit less dramatic than in the American data, emerged in the 1992 BCS. Afro–Caribbean victims are more likely to have been attacked and injured. They also tended to give high seriousness ratings to incidents in which they had been involved. These factors have the general effect of encouraging the reporting of personal crimes. Asians are somewhat disproportionately the victims of robbery and personal thefts (which are better reported), they are more likely than whites to be injured, and they suffered more property damage. Like Afro–Caribbeans, they gave the crimes in which they had been involved higher-seriousness ratings than did whites. This seems to account for the high level of crime reporting in Asians and average crime reporting levels in Afro-Caribbeans because, once these aspects of the crimes in which they had been involved are statistically equalised, both groups were less likely than whites to report having been victims of crime to the police. This difference is statistically significant only for Afro-Caribbeans, who are about six per cent less likely to report crime than might be expected, based on the other factors examined here (see below).

The BCS also asked ethnic minorities if they thought crimes against them had been racially motivated. Twelve per cent of crimes against Afro-Caribbeans were placed in this category, as were 24 per cent of crimes against Asians, but this experience did not have a significant additional effect on crime reporting.

Having had access to a telephone does not seem to have had much of an effect on crime reporting. As we saw above, the telephone was not the only way in which crimes had been reported. But it must often be the easiest way to contact the police, and telephone ownership has increased from 75 per cent to 88 per cent since the 1982 BCS. The percentage of incidents reported by phone has also increased (Mayhew and Aye Maung, 1992). But Table 4.5 shows that the difference in crime reporting between households that have telephones and those that do not is only about one percentage point. Access to a telephone is related to many other features of life that are also related to the reporting of crime: a prominent example is income. But, even when those factors are controlled for, the impact of telephone access on crime reporting remains insignificant.

Attitudes towards the police

Given the strained relationship between the police and some sections of the population, it seems likely that those who fear or distrust the police would be more hesitant to report crimes to them. Similarly, people who expect not to receive efficient or courteous service from the police might report crime less frequently, especially if other factors did not compel them to do so. But past research has found a surprisingly limited role for attitudes towards the police in victims' decision making. Often attitudes prove not to have been an important consideration, especially if the crimes were in any way serious.

Sparks, Genn and Dodd (1977) found only a very weak relationship between the reporting of crime and people's dislike of the police, their expectations of poor service, or bad experiences of the police, in their survey of inner-London neighbourhoods. Tuck and Southgate (1981) found that whites and Afro-Caribbeans reported having been victims of crime to the police at the same rate, despite large differences in their attitudes towards the police. American surveys have come to the same conclusion, even in places where dislike of the police is much more common than is typical of British communities.

This finding is often taken as further evidence that crime reporting largely reflects incident-based cost-benefit calculations; that is, that victims weigh such factors as injury and loss against the personal costs and risks, including inconvenience and fear of retaliation, associated with involving the police. But the evidence is flawed by the way in which surveys sequence their questions about crime reporting and attitudes towards the police.

Surveys inevitably ask about the reporting of past incidents, but their attitude measures invariably focus on the present. In this situation, people's attitudes may stem from having reported the crime and the events that followed but their attitudes may also have been a reason for reporting that crime to the police. As a result, although tabulations linking attitudes and crime reporting highlight a potentially important relationship, we cannot specify how that relationship works (Pease, 1988).

There is a link between people's attitudes and crime reporting in the BCS. When asked how good a job the police in their area did, people who thought their local police did a very good job had reported 53 per cent of offences. Victims in other categories, ranging from "fairly good job" to "very poor job", had reported an average of about 40 per cent of offences.

This was despite the fact that people who did not like the police were also more likely to have been victims of serious crimes, which were more frequently reported. Controlling for what people considered the seriousness of a crime does not change the equation very much; the 20-point seriousness rating had eight times the impact of attitude on reporting, which remained statistically significant but slight.

When respondents were asked why they had not reported crimes, sections of the population who rated police performance as poor more often said that they feared or disliked the police. Fear or dislike of the police was disproportionately cited by young, single, lower-income people, and by males and Afro-Caribbeans. This reason for the non-reporting of crime was, in fact, more closely linked to socio-economic factors than any other factor on the list.

One clear relationship in the 1992 BCS is that victims of more than one offence report crimes less often. Respondents were first asked about their experiences of crime in the previous year. They were then asked if they had been the victim of a burglary, assault, sexual assault or robbery, in the more distant past. Those who had been victims in the more distant past were less likely to report personal crimes that had happened more recently, but they were not less likely to report property crimes. This is illustrated in Table 4.5. Past victims were also likely to say that fear or dislike of the police was the reason why they had not reported incidents.

Multivariate analysis

This discussion has highlighted the complexity of forces affecting the reporting of crimes to the police. The relationship between victims and offenders, the distribution of injury and financial loss, the locations in which crimes take place, family income and other factors are linked to one another as well as to the reporting of crime. This complexity of factors often suppresses, but may also magnify, the apparent link between reporting and any particular explanatory factor.

This section attempts to isolate the most important of the factors affecting the reporting of crime. It uses multivariate logistic regression to predict which incidents in the 1992 BCS had been reported and which had not, and uses the kinds of evaluation measures described in Tables 4.2 to 4.5. The results are presented in Table 4.6.

Table 4.6 presents estimates of the effect of each of the explanatory variables on the probability that incidents had been reported to the police. The probability column shows the change in the likelihood of a crime being reported that is associated with the incident being in one category or another of each of the explanatory variables. The measures of probability range from 0 to 1. The explanatory variables in Table 4.6 are all dichotomies (scored from 0 to 1), with two exceptions. These exceptions are: the value of stolen property and reported damage (scaled in multiples of £10), and the location's size, which is ordered in five categories (rural, mixed, urban, metropolitan and inner-city).

The estimates of changes in the likelihood of reporting that are presented in Table 4.6 hold when all of the other explanatory variables are at their average value, which is equivalent to saying "when everything else is normal" (for a discussion see Peterson, 1985). For example, if everything else is normal (all the other explanatory variables are at their average value), each additional loss of £10 is estimated to increase reporting by 1.1 per cent. If someone had been injured seriously enough to need the attention of a doctor or hospital, the estimated likelihood that the crime would have been reported rises 15.2 per cent. Table 4.6 presents only factors that proved to be statistically significant. (To account for the design effects inherent in the BCS a $p \leq .04$ test was used to identify reliable relationships.)

Crimes that had been reported by victims to someone other than the police are excluded from the analysis. Like all the analyses in this chapter that include race, Table 4.6 uses the ethnic minority booster sample, which increases the total number of cases on which the analysis is based to 649 Asians and 748 Afro-Caribbeans.

Table 4.6 shows the importance of what respondents felt to be the degree of intrusiveness of the crime to their reporting of that crime. Separate measures of home location, whether the intruder had entered the home as opposed to an attempted entry or the burglary of a

Table 4.6
Multivariate Analysis of Crime Reporting

Explanatory Variables	Change in Probability
Offender Intrusiveness	
location – home	.053
offender right to be there	.088
actual home intrusion	.063
job related offence	.055
Seriousness of the Threat	
weapon was present	.056
Financial Consequences	
value stolen (per £10)	.011
damage value (per £10)	.005
had insured property loss	.073
crime a car theft	.176
Personal Impact	
had an emotional reaction	.047
injury-doctor or hospital	.152
Victim-Offender Relationship	
seen or casually known	.034
relative or partner	-.135
Victim Background	
over 60 years old	.034
home owner	.027
council resident	.043
Afro-Caribbean	-.044
Urbanism category	-.010

Core and ethnic booster sample, unweighted data. Based on first three victim forms only; excludes out of scope incidents and incidents reported to other authorities. Based on 6053 complete-data cases. All coefficients were evaluated at their means. R^2(pseudo)=.26.

garage, and whether or not the offender had had a right to be at the scene when the crime happened were all linked to the reporting of crimes. The threat to safety signalled by the presence of a weapon had about the same effect as an intrusion into the home. But, net of the other factors here, crimes involving only attacks and threats were not especially likely to have been reported.

All of the financial consequences of crime were linked to higher levels of reporting, as were emotional impact and serious physical injury. Offences committed by offenders whom victims knew <u>something</u> about (they had "seen them around", as they put it, or had known them casually) were slightly more than three per cent more likely to have been brought to the attention of the police than offences committed by strangers or unknown parties. Crimes involving relatives, marital partners and former partners, were less likely to have been reported, by almost 14 per cent. Crimes committed by offenders who were well known to the victim, such as neighbours, colleagues, clients, acquaintances and local youths, had been reported at about the same rate as crimes committed by strangers. That coefficient is therefore excluded from Table 4.6. Older people were more likely to report crimes; both home owners and residents of council housing were more likely than private tenants to report crime, after allowing for other factors; and Afro-Caribbeans were less likely to report offences to the police.

Table 4.6 excludes a number of factors that were not significantly related to crime reporting once they had been taken into account. There was no evidence that access to a telephone had encouraged the reporting of crime. Having had a child at home (which was related to having taken crime-prevention measures) was not related to reporting, nor was having been a victim in the past or the victim of a recurring crime. Injuries that had fallen short of needing medical attention were not especially likely to be reported. Women generally get along better with the police but they were not more likely than men to report crime; and the reporting of crime by Asians was not significantly different from that of whites.

Which survey company had conducted the interview also had no effect. Nor had income, having been a victim in the past or victim culpability. Social class, unemployment and whether the victim felt the offence had been racially motivated, were excluded because they masked the impact of other factors to which they were highly related. Whether a crime fell into the personal or property category was included in the analysis summarised in Table 4.6 but, once other factors had been taken into account, it had not relationship to the reporting of crime.

The variables summarised in Table 4.6 correctly classified 74 per cent of all offences as either reported or not reported. The variables also correctly classified 89 per cent of the incidents that had, in fact, not been reported but they were less successful at predicting which incidents *had been* reported; they correctly classified 57 per cent of those incidents, but cast 43 per cent into the unreported category.

The variables did not account for the reporting of a large number of crimes. Among frequently occurring crimes, the variables greatly under-predicted the reporting of bicycle thefts. Such variables as intrusion, value of loss, insurance and other measures predicted that 47 per cent of bicycle thefts would be reported, but victims said that 69 per cent of such offences had been brought to the attention of the police. Perhaps respondents who had had their bicycles stolen expected that reporting the offence would aid the recovery of their property.

The factors listed in Table 4.6 also under-predicted the reporting of burglaries that had not resulted in a loss; they predicted that 58 per cent would be reported, but, in fact, 73 per cent of such burglaries had been reported. On the other hand, the variables over-predicted the reporting of vehicle vandalism by projecting that 27 per cent would be reported; but only 9 per cent actually had been. They also over-predicted theft in a dwelling, probably because of the location and financial loss incurred.

Car theft, which had been reported in 99 per cent of cases, was accurately classified only by including a special measure that identified those cases. The extraordinary reporting rate for this offence is not fully captured by the high value of the typical loss, or by insurance. The reporting of car theft is probably further stimulated by factors such as the high recovery rate for stolen cars; in the 1992 BCS, 72 per cent of car-theft victims said that their vehicle had later been recovered and almost half had been recovered within 24 hours. Car theft can also impose a great deal of inconvenience on victims' everyday lives. In all, such unmeasured features of car theft accounted for an estimated increase of 17.6 per cent in reporting (the value of the special coefficient in Table 4.6 for vehicle theft).

Conclusion

This chapter described many factors that had been involved in decisions by victims to report crimes to the police. It confirmed that crime reporting was very responsive to the seriousness of the incident. The reporting of crime was driven by the intrusiveness of crime, the threat the crime had posed for the personal safety of victims, the extent of injury and loss it had entailed and its emotional impact.

But more than the seriousness of the incident was involved. Using the 0-20 scale against which victims were asked to rate the seriousness of each incident, Mayhew et al. (1993) found that 38 per cent of the most serious crimes had not been reported, but that 25 per cent of the most trivial crimes had been reported. Many reasons for the under-reporting of serious crime have been examined in this report. Culpable victims tended to report less frequently, as did those with past experiences of crime. Afro-Caribbeans were less willing to report crimes to the police, no matter what the situation in which they found themselves and in spite of their tending to be the victims of more serious crime.

Crimes whose perpetrators had had some link to their victims (as relatives, partners, friends and neighbours) had also often gone unreported. A disproportionate number of these victims of related-party crimes had suffered violent assault. These victims had also suffered the bulk of injury-inflicting crimes uncovered by the BCS. Eighty per cent of all personal crimes involving people who were related to one another had led to injury, and a third of those had called for a doctor's attention. Twenty per cent of the victims of unreported violent assault cited fear of reprisal as the reason for not having reported the crime.

This chapter also explored a number of reasons why many less serious incidents had been reported. These incidents are important partly because they were so numerous. Using the rating cut off employed by Mayhew *et al.* (1993), 40 per cent of crimes uncovered in the 1992 BCS were judged as relatively trivial. Even though only 25 per cent of these crimes had been reported, they still constituted a large percentage of the workload facing the police. One important factor leading to the reporting of less serious crimes is insurance.

The increasing scope of insurance coverage in the population may also explain the increase in property-crime reporting over the years. Since 1988 alone, the percentage of BCS offences covered by insurance has increased from 37 per cent to 50 per cent (Mayhew & Aye Maung, 1992). Insurance coverage increases the likelihood of a crime being reported by an estimated 7.3 per cent. In light of this effect, insurance coverage certainly plays an important role in explaining rising rates of recorded crime, especially burglary. Crime reporting, independent of the seriousness of the crime, was also higher among older victims and home owners, both growing sections of the population.

5 Conclusions

This is an era of rapid change for policing. Alterations are being proposed in police organisation and governance that are intended to increase policy efficiency and effectiveness. As part of this process, police forces have had to open themselves to public inspection as never before, and many have responded quickly. Her Majesty's Inspectorate of Constabulary (HMIC) has outlined a list of workload and performance indicators that it will collect and publish, and the Audit Commission has added several more. Audit Commission guidelines call for the yearly publication of police force performance indicators by the end of 1994. Forces are being asked to set performance targets, and whether or not they have met them will be more visible.

As this is occurring, expectations about what the police should be doing have also been changing. For example, the Victims' Charter that was issued by the Home Office in 1990 describes how victims can expect to be treated by the police, and what kinds of service victims are entitled to receive from the criminal justice system. This emphasis on the consumers or customers of the police service is also called for in the Citizen's Charter. This drive to clarify the relationship between the police and the public can be seen in management changes in the police service that are designed to fix responsibility for decision making closer to the point where officers meet the public.

Surveys of the public's opinion and experience of crime and of the police have become an integral part of this shift towards greater police accountability to the public. Some forces are conducting surveys of their direct clientele, including victims, people who report accidents and visitors to police stations. Others are surveying residents of higher-crime areas to probe their views about what actions the police should take, as well as gathering reports of what happens when these local people call for assistance.

The Home Office, HMIC and the Association of Chief Police Officers (ACPO) are trying to encourage and standardise the quality of these efforts. These surveys are, of course, additions to the usual ways that the police gauge community opinion, which include local consultation panels, Neighbourhood Watch groups, tenants associations and organisations representing members of the community.

Interestingly, this survey initiative is not confined to Britain. Similar soundings of public opinion are being conducted in Australia, the United States and Canada, as part of a move towards community policing. Surveys are not an absolute source of wisdom for police priorities. They do not address such issues as the honesty and integrity of officers and they do not shed much light on how to cut the costs of the police service, because the public usually wants more police service, not less. But surveys can identify areas in which the priorities of the police and the public differ.

The results of BCS, as well as local surveys, can also be used to provide feedback about performance in areas that are of concern to police managers and local Police Authorities. The first of these areas is crime. The BCS gives some answers to such basic questions as: How much crime is there? How many crimes are coming to the attention of the police? What are the police doing about these crimes?

Mayhew, *et al.* (1993) give detailed answers to the first question. They report that the number of crime victims has increased significantly since the 1988 BCS, but less so than officially recorded crime. One reason for this disjuncture is that crime reporting by victims increased and thus magnified official statistics. Accordingly, Chapter 4 examined the factors involved in the decision by victims to report crimes to the police.

Crime reporting was principally determined by the seriousness of crime. The more incidents intruded into the privacy of victims' homes, threatened their personal safety, led to injury or financial loss or exacted an emotional toll, the more likely crimes were to be reported. Afro-Caribbeans proved less willing to report crimes to the police once the seriousness of the crimes to which they had fallen victim was taken into account. Finally, a disproportionate number of violent assaults and crimes inflicting injury turned out to involve perpetrators who were relatives, partners, friends or neighbours of their victims. These crimes also often went unreported.

A second issue of concern to police managers is how well the police are handling calls for service from the public. The volume of requests for information and help has been rising much faster than anticipated and is challenging the capacity of the police to respond with equal vigour to all demands for their attention. One problem this generates is a potential discrepancy between the public's expectation of rapid police response and the understanding among those within policing circles that many calls for service are not emergencies and do not require the police to respond rapidly, and that many such calls do not require the personal presence of a uniformed officer at all.

The need to husband police resources has led to the widespread adoption of graded response schemes that sometimes bar the dispatch of patrol cars, or send them some time later. Opinion polls show that such schemes are not endorsed by the public. In 1989, three-quarters of the respondents to a national survey thought that all crimes deserve equal attention and that responding rapidly to calls should be a high priority for the police (Joint Consultative Committee, 1990).

When BCS respondents contacted the police to report crimes that involved them or other people, their experience was mixed. Shapland, *et al.* (1985) argue that victims' needs are as follows: they want a prompt visit, attention to their plight, support on the scene, referrals to sources of further assistance and information about the progress of their case. Some of these standards had usually been met when people had called about a crime, but others had not. Most people were happy with the speed with which the police had responded, and even more felt they had been treated courteously.

But about one-third felt that the police had not given their problem as much attention or effort as it deserved, and only a quarter felt they had been kept informed about the progress of their case. In all, victims were the least satisfied of all those contacting the police. They were, in fact, less satisfied with their experience than those who had been stopped in a vehicle or on foot. Of those who called to report a crime, the most disgruntled were victims of serious crimes and victims of more than one crime.

But Mayhew, *et al.* (1993) report that the decline in satisfaction registered by victims between 1984 and 1988 has mostly been made up by increases in satisfaction since then. Levels of satisfaction among victims in the 1992 BCS are only slightly below the 1984 levels. The BCS and other surveys suggest that 1988 may have been the low point in public opinion of the police.

The police are also concerned about their ability to handle contacts with the public in an even-handed manner. ACPO notes that people rightly expect "... the highest possible standard of fairness, courtesy and sensitivity in the behaviour of officers with whom they come into contact..." and identifies this as "an essential requirement of the Police Service" (ACPO, 1990). The BCS suggests that most police-initiated encounters had been handled courteously, outright impoliteness by the police had been quite rare, and that the bulk of respondents felt they had been treated fairly. A significant number of respondents involved in car stops felt that the police had not taken enough interest in what they had to say on their own behalf, but very few racial minorities were annoyed about racist language or behaviour by police officers.

The quality of service people had received was linked to their background. Asians and Afro-Caribbeans were twice as likely to report that they had had to wait an unreasonable length of time for the police to respond, and they were less likely to think the police had taken appropriate interest in their case or that the police had put enough effort into it. Asians were particularly unlikely to report that the police had been very polite. Younger people who had contacted the police were also much less likely to report that the police had given their complaint enough attention or that the police had been interested in what they had had to say; younger people were also less likely to think they had been treated politely.

Dense traffic presents problems for motorists and for the police. The police traditionally spend much time investigating and reporting accidents, as well as allocating many officers to traffic enforcement duty. The 1992 BCS suggests that traffic enforcement has increased because significantly more people than in 1988 had been stopped while driving. Respondents' assessments of the police's handling of traffic problems were positive, especially in groups that are less likely to drive a great deal, and those living outside of inner London. But traffic control is fairly low on the public's agenda. A survey for the Joint Consultative Committee (1990) found that respondents gave the enforcement of traffic regulations and maintenance of road safety only half the importance they gave to preventing crime, and those duties fell to the bottom of a list of seven police responsibilities respondents were asked to prioritise.

Police managers are increasingly urged to consult and become involved with the community. The 1992 BCS indicates that many people are uncertain about how good a job the police do in working with groups in the community, but that those with an opinion were fairly favourable. Most of those questioned thought the police did a good job giving advice on how to prevent crime. But victims of personal and property crimes, and respondents who perceived high levels of physical decay and social disorder in their area, were among those who did not think the police made a good job of relating to the community.

What many members of the public are looking for is <u>reassurance</u> that they are being protected. This reassurance comes in many forms. For victims, it is given by the police responding quickly and by their being supportive. Some people want the police to concentrate more on public disorder such as public drinking and noisy teenagers; others want an end to racially motivated attacks. For many, seeing the police patrolling the streets sends a reassuring message that the police, if needed, are on hand.

One of the most important points of contact between the public and the police is routine patrolling. It is clear from surveys and other indices of opinion that many people want to see the police patrolling more often, and especially on foot. Much dissatisfaction with current levels of foot patrol was expressed in the 1992 BCS; 61 per cent of respondents felt the police did a fairly or very poor job at it. About one-quarter felt the same about police patrolling in cars. The BCS found that seven per cent of respondents recalled having seen a police officer patrolling on foot very recently ("today or yesterday"), and about 20 per cent within the past week.

Foot patrols were more visible in inner city and metropolitan areas throughout England and Wales, and especially in London. Young, single people and Afro-Caribbeans, had also often seen the police patrolling on foot. These respondents were, for other reasons, among those who were most dissatisfied with policing. Respondents from lower risk areas and smaller jurisdictions had seen police patrolling on foot less often.

Police visibility was related to higher levels of satisfaction with policing among whites and Asians but not among Afro-Caribbeans and only slightly among younger men. Afro-

Caribbeans and younger men frequently recalled having seen police patrolling on foot, but their experiences of the police had not been the most satisfactory.

For most people, seeing the police patrolling on foot was related to satisfaction across a broad set of performance measures, even when other important determinants of attitudes to the police were taken into account. The popularity of foot patrol is an instance in which pressure for greater police effectiveness can run counter to public expectations. Foot patrolling is expensive to mount, it is often in competition for the staffing needed to respond rapidly to 999 calls (which the public also wants), and does not register well on performance indices such as making arrests and clearing up crimes.

Research suggests that foot patrol's biggest impact is the reassurance it provides, and that it reduces fear of crime. Foot patrol may be the issue that most clearly highlights the potential clash between popular and administrative concerns. It certainly presents a hard set of choices for police forces pressed on one side to reduce costs and control the growth of personnel, and on the other to respond to the expectations of very large sections of the public who want a visible police service.

Appendix A
A note on public opinion measures

The trend in public opinion shown in Figure 2.1 was based on respondents who expressed an opinion about the police, and excluded respondents who said they did not know how good a job the police were doing. Surveys of opinion about policing frequently find that many people refrain from expressing an opinion, especially when they are asked about specific aspects of police work.

As Chapter 2 reports, survey questions that examine task-specific assessments of police performance find that "don't know" responses rise to as high as 31 per cent when respondents are asked about lower-visibility issues such as the police's effectiveness in dealing with white-collar crime. The general measure of performance examined in Chapter 2 ("how good a job...?") elicited fewer such answers, but that percentage varied considerably depending on the year the survey was conducted and by whom. As detailed in Appendix B, the percentage of BCS respondents who said they did not know how good a job their local police were doing ranged from 19 per cent (1982) to 7 per cent (1984), and from 13 per cent (1988) to 15 per cent (1992). The "don't know" figures for the Gallup surveys were lower, ranging from 9 to 11 per cent.

The distribution of "don't know" responses appears to be a function of differences in how the various survey organisations dealt with respondents who did not express an opinion. Survey organisations can differ in how hard their interviewers are expected to press for firm answers, and interviewers vary in carrying out this assignment. For example, Gallup questionnaires do not list "don't know" responses as possible answers, and they are recorded only at the insistence of the respondent.

The impact a survey organisation may have on the results of a survey can be illustrated by the two surveys conducted in early 1992: the BCS and the first Gallup survey of the year. They were conducted at almost the same time, but Gallup's "don't know" figure was 60 per cent lower (9 per cent against 15 per cent). On the other hand, there were no significant differences between the rates of "don't know" responses for the two companies that shared the interviewing for the 1992 BCS. When such procedural variations are present, they make it difficult to interpret trends based on all respondents. Nevertheless, the pattern among those with an opinion seems clear.

The significant number of "don't know" responses to questions about particular aspects of police performance also played a role in decisions about how to construct attitudinal scales assessing opinion. Chapters 2 and 3 make use of an overall performance assessment measure that is based on responses to all 13 questions described in Table 2.1. Each respondent's score is a sum of the aspects of police performance that they were willing to rate. The score was then standardised to account for differences in the number of responses that went into calculating it. The internal consistency of this general index was high among the 2,480 respondents who responded to all of the items, and the reliability of the score (based on Cronbach's Alpha) was +.84.

Because of patterns in the extent of non-response, the scores less often reflect opinions about white-collar crime, service to crime victims, working with the community and other aspects of police performance that had high rates of "don't know" responses. But the number of items that respondents were willing to respond to were virtually uncorrelated ($r = -.02$) with their overall scores. Respondents with extensive experience of the police were more likely to respond to more of the questions, including those who had been stopped or who had contacted the police, those who had been sanctioned and those who had been crime victims. Respondents with less education were less likely than others to express opinions.

A related issue is the reliability and validity of measures of public opinion about the police. Over a decade, the BCS and related surveys have questioned respondents about how good a job they felt the police were doing. That trend data is examined in Chapter 2. But to what extent have the surveys assessed considered and firmly held beliefs as opposed to casual responses to unfamiliar questionnaire items? Much of this report has focused on reports of specific encounters with the police, for just this reason.

It is important to note that the question concerning how good a job the police were doing was positioned to maximise the extent to which it measured considered opinion. In the 1992 BCS, this question follows: (a) intensive questioning of respondents about their experiences as crime victims, including what happened if they reported a crime to the police; and (b) 67 detailed questions about the experiences that respondents recalled having had of the police, including whether they had been stopped by the police or had called them for help. This question was similarly positioned in the 1988 BCS.

The 13 questions about specific aspects of police performance that were included in the 1992 BCS came after the general "how good a job...?" question, so those questions were also positioned to reflect respondents' experiences. The Gallup surveys discussed in Chapter 2 were also structured to open with questions about respondents' contact with and experiences of the police, before moving to general evaluative questions.

Did this question sequence make a difference? To evaluate this, the 1992 BCS asked respondents twice about how good a job they felt the police did. The question was first asked very early in the interview, following a few warm-up questions about respondents' neighbourhoods and fear of crime. The question was then repeated much later in the questionnaire, as described above. A comparison of responses shows that there was some shift in opinion, but that opinion was generally fairly stable. Responses to the two questions were correlated +.74.

Interestingly, what shift in opinion there was during the course of the interview was in a positive direction. Among those who responded to both questions, the percentage of people who said that the police did a very good or fairly good job increased by almost six percentage points after respondents completed the intervening sequence of questions.

The largest shift was among those who rated police performance as fairly poor at the beginning; 31 per cent of those respondents chose more positive response categories later in the interview. There was also a very slight decline (1.3 per cent) in the frequency of "don't know" responses. The analyses presented in this report used responses to the second of the questions because its positioning in the sequence of questions more closely resembled past BCS questionnaires.

Appendix B
Detailed tabulations of survey results

Table B.1
Trends in Attitudes Toward Police

	Per cent Including Don't Know					Per cent ~~Including~~ Excluding Don't Know				
Survey	very good	fairly good	fairly poor	very poor	don't know	very good	fairly good	fairly poor	very poor	Cases
BCS 01/82	35	40	5	2	19	43	49	6	2	6307
BCS 01/84	31	52	7	2	7	34	56	8	3	6582
BCS 01/88	22	53	9	3	13	25	61	10	4	4906
OPCS 12/90	22	50	8	5	15	26	59	9	6	1622
Gallup 08/91	23	52	11	6	9	25	57	13	6	1844
Gallup 10/91	25	51	9	6	10	27	56	10	6	1893
BCS 01/92	20	49	11	5	15	24	58	13	6	5038
Gallup 01/92	24	54	9	4	9	27	59	10	4	2003
Gallup 04/92	21	54	10	4	11	23	61	11	5	1892
Gallup 10/92	21	53	12	5	9	23	58	13	5	1927

Weighted core samples; unweighted case counts are given.

Table B.2
Contacts Initiated By The Public

Type of Contact (One or More Times)	Per cent
To report a crime of which you or someone in your household was a victim	13.1
To report a crime of which someone else was the victim	4.2
Because you were told or asked to do so (e.g. to show documents, give a statement)	3.6
To report a traffic accident or medical emergency	3.9
To report a burglar alarm ringing	2.8
To report a car alarm going off	0.4
To report any other suspicious circumstances or persons	5.6
To report any type of disturbance, noise or nuisance (apart from alarms going off)	3.7
To report a missing person	0.4
To report that you had lost something (including animals)	3.2
To report that you had found something (including animals)	3.1
To tell them that your home was going to be empty	1.7
To report any other type of problem or difficulty	3.2
To ask for directions or the time	2.6
To ask for any other sort of advice or information	3.9
To give them any other sort of information	3.5
Just for a social chat	2.3
Total unweighted cases	5184

Weighted data, half core sample. These are the categories listed on a show card presented to respondents.

Table B.3
Social Correlates of Contacts With Police

Social Background	Per cent Contacting Police	Per cent Stopped by Police	Per cent Visited by Police	Unweighted Cases
Race				
white	40	22	13	4925
Afro-Caribbean	32	36	13	93
Asian	30	22	13	109
Household Income				
less than £10,000	31	19	10	2191
£10,000-£19,999	44	22	15	1299
£20,000 or more	50	29	18	1115
Housing Tenure*				
home owners	40	22	13	3592
council housing	34	16	11	1059
private rental	41	25	20	480
Sex				
males	43	28	15	2360
females	36	16	12	2816
Marital Status				
unmarried	35	26	13	2134
married	42	20	14	3018
Family Status				
have children	46	27	18	1533
no children	36	19	12	3637
Labour Force Status				
unemployed	45	35	16	289
all others	39	21	13	4860
Household Vehicles				
have car or cycle	42	24	14	3833
all others	26	11	12	1343
Victimisation				
victim of any type	53	29	17	2145
non-victims	28	16	11	2954
Age Category				
16-19	30	46	14	208
20-29	50	36	16	840
30-39	46	26	18	1007
40-49	47	23	14	827
50-59	41	15	13	669
60 and older	23	6	8	1604
Total	39	22	14	5176

Core sample; weighted data. This table follows the categories presented in Table 3.1. Stopped by police includes traffic and pedestrian stops, orders to show documents or give a statement, and other police-initiated contacts in which respondents were under suspicion. Visits by police include contacts to return missing property, to ask for information, etc. * indicates small "other" categories are excluded from the table. "Don't know" or other non-responses are excluded in every case, most notably for household income.

Table B.4
Nature of Contact and Extent of Dissatisfaction with Encounters
Initiated by the Public

Description of Contact	Contact about crime		Contact about alarms, suspicion		Unweighted Cases
	Bit/very dissatisfied	Less favourable	Bit/very dissatisfied	Less favourable	Crime-Other
How long waited before the police attended to the matter?					
no wait	20	5	8	4	74–69
reasonable time	22	11	18	7	61–49
not reasonable time	79	30	76	25	31–30
How much interest in what you had to say?					
as much as should	15	2	8	5	124–120
less than they should	73	38	74	25	50–38
How much effort police put into dealing with the matter?					
as much as should	13	1	2	2	109–102
less than they should	74	34	80	31	54–42
How well did [police] keep you informed about what was happening					
very/fairly well	6	1	6	3	49–32
not very/ not at all well	50	22	31	12	81–81
How polite were they in dealing with you?					
very polite	21	7	12	4	127–127
fairly polite	56	17	35	15	41–41
fairly/very impolite	100	90	94	100	5–8

Weighted data, half core sample. Number of cases is for the "unfavourable" measure. This table does not report data for contacts involving asking for or giving information, or social contacts.

Table B-5
Nature of Contact and Extent of Dissatisfaction with Encounters
Initiated by the Police

Description of Contact	Vehicle Stops		Pedestrian Stops		Cases
	Bit/very dissatisfied	Less favourable	Bit/very dissatisfied	Less favourable	Vehicle- Other
Did the officer give a reason for stopping you?					
no	37	18	48	32	65–29
yes	17	11	29	17	672–103
Were respondent, others or vehicle searched?					
no	17	11	30	17	692–100
yes	35	17	44	34	54–32
Was someone arrested, breath-tested, issued a vehicle or fixed penalty notice, told to take documents to a police station, have their name and address taken, searched, or prosecuted?					
no	10	7	31	14	449–82
yes	31	68	36	30	297–50
How much interest in what you had to say?					
as much as should	9	6	21	14	258–89
less than they should	37	22	70	39	424–33
How polite were they in dealing with you?					
very/fairly polite	11	7	18	11	629–104
fairly/very impolite	69	42	88	54	105–28

Weighted data, half core sample. Number of cases is for the "unfavourable" measure.

References

Association of Chief Police Officers. (1990). *Setting the Standards for Policing: Meeting Community Expectations.* London.

Burrows, J. (1986). *Burglary: Police Actions and Victim's Views.* Research and Planning Unit Paper No. 37. London: Home Office.

Ekblom, P. and Heal, K. (1982). *The Police Response to Calls From the Public.* Research and Planning Unit Paper No. 9. London: Home Office.

Gallup Ltd. (1992). *Gallup Political and Economic Index*, Report Number 388. London.

Hough, M. (1989). 'Demand for policing and police performance: progress and pitfalls in public surveys'. In Weatheritt, M. (Ed.), *Police Research: some future prospects.* Farnborough: Avebury.

Joint Consultative Committee (1990). *The Operational Policing Review.* Surbiton: The Joint Consultative Committee of the three Police Staff Associations of England and Wales.

Jones, T., Maclean, B. and Young, J. (1986). *The Islington Crime Survey.* Aldershot: Gower.

Maxfield, M. (1988). 'The London Metropolitan Police and their clients: victim and suspect attitudes'. *Journal of Research in Crime and Delinquency, 25*, pp. 188-206.

Mayhew, P. and Aye Maung, N. (1992). 'Surveying crime: findings from the 1992 British Crime Survey'. Home Office Research and Statistics Department: *Research Findings, 2*, pp. 1-6.

Mayhew, P. Aye Maung, N. and Mirrlees-Black, C. (1993). *The 1992 British Crime Survey.* Home Office Research Study No. 132. London: HMSO.

Mayhew P. and Elliott, D. (1990). 'Self-reported offending, victimisation, and the British Crime Survey'. *Violence and Victims, 5*, pp. 83-96.

McConville, M. and Shepherd, D. (1992). Watching Police, *Watching Communities.* London: Routledge.

Pease, K. (1988). *Judgments of Crime Seriousness: Evidence from the 1984 BCS.* Research and Planning Unit Paper No. 44. London: Home Office.

Peterson, T. (1985). 'A comment on presenting results from logit and probit models'. *American Sociological Review, 50*, 131-131.

Ramsay, M. (1991). 'Restricting public drinking: studies by the Home Office and two local authorities'. *Home Office Research Bulletin, 30*, 16-20.

Shah, R. and Pease, K. (1992). "Crime, race and reporting to the police". *The Howard Journal, 31*, 192-199.

Shapland, J. Wilmore, J. and Duff, P. (1985). *Victims in the Criminal Justice System*. Aldershot: Gower.

Shapland, J. and Vagg, J. (1987). 'Using the police'. *British Journal of Criminology*, 27, 54-73.

Skogan, W. (1984). 'Reporting crimes to police: the status of world research'. *Journal of Research in Crime and Delinquency,* 21, pp. 113-137.

Skogan, W. (1990). *The Police and Public in England and Wales*. Home Office Research Study No. 117. London: HMSO.

Smith, D. (1983). *Police and People in London: A Survey of Londoners*. London: Policy Studies Institute.

Southgate, P. and Crisp, D. (1992). *Public Satisfaction with Police Services*. Research and Planning Unit Paper No. 73. London: Home Office.

Sparks, R., Genn H. and Dodd, D. (1977). *Surveying Victims*. London: John Wiley.

Tuck, M. and Southgate, P. (1981). *Ethnic Minorities, Crime and Policing: A Survey of the Experiences of West Indians and Whites*. Home Office Research Study No. 70. London: HMSO.

Publications

List of Research and Planning Unit publications

The Research and Planning Unit (previously the Research Unit) has been publishing its work since 1955, and a full list of papers is provided below. These reports are available on request from the Home Office Research and Planning Unit, Information Section, Room 278, 50 Queen Anne's Gate, London SW1H 9AT. Telephone: 071-273 2084 (answerphone).

Reports published in the HORS series are available from HMSO, who will advise as to prices, at the following address: :

HMSO Publications Centre

PO Box 276

London SW8 5DT

Telephone orders: 071-873 9090

General enquiries: 071-873 0011

Titles already published for the Home Office
Studies in the Causes of Delinquency and the Treatment of Offenders (SCDTO)

1. Prediction methods in relation to borstal training. Hermann Mannheim and Leslie T. Wilkins. 1955. viii + 276pp. (11 340051 9)

2. Time spent awaiting trial. Evelyn Gibson. 1960. v + 45pp. (34-368-2).

3. Delinquent generations. Leslie T. Wilkins. 1960. iv + 20pp. (11 340053 5).

4. Murder. Evelyn Gibson and S. Klein. 1961. iv + 44pp. (11 340054 3).

5. Persistent criminals. A study of all offenders liable to preventive detention in 1956. W.H. Hammond and Edna Chayen. 1963. ix + 237pp.(34-368-5).

6. Some statistical and other numerical techniques for classifying individuals. P. McNaughton-Smith. 1965. v + 33pp (34-368-6).

7. Probation research: a preliminary report. Part I. General outline of research. Part II. Study of Middlesex probation area (SOMPA) Steven Folkard, Kate Lyon, Margaret M. Carver and Erica O'Leary. 1966.vi + 58pp. (11 340374 7).

8. Probation research: national study of probation. Trends and regional comparisons in probation (England and Wales). Hugh Barr and Erica O'Leary. 1966. vii + 51pp. (34-368-8).

9.   Probation research. A survey of group work in the probation service. Hugh Barr. 1966. vii + 94pp. (34-368-9).

10.   Types of delinquency and home background. A validation study of Hewitt and Jenkins' hypothesis. Elizabeth Field. 1967. vi + 21pp. (34-368-10).

11.   Studies of female offenders. No. 1 - Girls of 16-20 years sentenced to borstal or detention centre training in 1963. No. 2 - Women offenders in the Metropolitan Police District in March and April 1957. No. 3 - A description of women in prison on January 1, 1965. Nancy Goodman and Jean Price. 1967. v + 78pp. (34-368-11).

12.   The use of the Jesness Inventory on a sample of British probationers. Martin Davies. 1967. iv + 20pp. (34-368-12).

13.   The Jesness Inventory: application to approved school boys. Joy Mott. 1969. iv + 27pp. (11 340063 2).

Home Office Research Studies (HORS)

(Nos 1–106 are out of print)

1.   Workloads in children's departments. Eleanor Grey. 1969. vi + 75pp. (11 340101 9).

2.   Probationers in their social environment. A study of male probationers aged 17-20, together with an analysis of those reconvicted within twelve months. Martin Davies. 1969. vii + 204pp. (11 340102 7).

3.   Murder 1957 to 1968. A Home Office Statistical Division report on murder in England and Wales. Evelyn Gibson and S. Klein (with annex by the Scottish Home and Health Department on murder in Scotland). 1969. vi + 94pp. (11 340103 5).

4.   Firearms in crime. A Home Office Statistical Division report on indictable offences involving firearms in England and Wales. A. D. Weatherhead and B. M. Robinson. 1970. viii + 39pp. (11 340104 3).

5.   Financial penalties and probation. Martin Davies. 1970. vii + 39pp. (11 340105 1).

6.   Hostels for probationers. A study of the aims, working and variations in effectiveness of male probation hostels with special reference to the influence of the environment on delinquency. Ian Sinclair. 1971 x + 200pp. (11 340106 X).

7.   Prediction methods in criminology - including a prediction study of young men on probation. Frances H. Simon. 1971. xi + 234pp.(11 340107 8).

8.   Study of the juvenile liaison scheme in West Ham 1961-65. Marilyn Taylor. 1971. vi + 46pp. (11 340108 6).

9.   Explorations in after-care. I - After-care units in London, Liverpool and Manchester. Martin Silberman (Royal London Prisoners' Aid Society) and Brenda Chapman.   II - After-care hostels receiving a Home Office

grant. Ian Sinclair and David Snow (HORU). III - St. Martin of Tours House, Aryeh Leissner (National Bureau for Co-operation in Child Care). 1971. xi + 140pp. (11 340109 4).

10.   A survey of adoption in Great Britain. Eleanor Grey in collaboration with Ronald M. Blunden. 1971. ix + 168pp. (11 340110 8).

11.   Thirteen-year-old approved school boys in 1962s. Elizabeth Field, W H Hammond and J. Tizard. 1971. ix + 46pp. (11 340111 6).

12.   Absconding from approved schools. R. V. G. Clarke and D. N. Martin. 1971. vi + 146pp.(11 340112 4).

13.   An experiment in personality assessment of young men remanded in custody. H. Sylvia Anthony. 1972. viii + 79pp. (11 340113 2).

14.   Girl offenders aged 17-20 years. I - Statistics relating to girl offenders aged 17-20 years from 1960 to 1970. II - Re-offending by girls released from borstal or detention centre training. III - The problems of girls released from borstal training during their period on after-care. Jean Davies and Nancy Goodman. 1972. v + 77pp. (11 340114 0).

15.   The controlled trial in institutional research - paradigm or pitfall for penal evaluators? R. V. G. Clarke and D. B. Cornish. 1972. v + 33pp. (11 340115 9).

16.   A survey of fine enforcement. Paul Softley. 1973. v + 65pp. (11 340116 7).

17.   An index of social environment - designed for use in social work research. Martin Davies. 1973. vi + 63pp. (11 340117 5).

18.   Social enquiry reports and the probation service. Martin Davies and Andrea Knopf. 1973. v + 49pp.(11 340118 3).

19.   Depression, psychopathic personality and attempted suicide in a borstal sample. H. Sylvia Anthony.1973. viii + 44pp. (0 11 340119 1).

20.   The use of bail and custody by London magistrates' courts before and after the Criminal Justice Act 1967. Frances Simon and Mollie Weatheritt. 1974. vi + 78pp. (0 11 340120 5).

21.   Social work in the environment. A study of one aspect of probation practice. Martin Davies, with Margaret Rayfield, Alaster Calder and Tony Fowles. 1974. ix + 151pp. (0 11 340121 3).

22.   Social work in prison. An experiment in the use of extended contact with offenders. Margaret Shaw.1974. viii + 154pp. (0 11 340122 1).

23.   Delinquency amongst opiate users. Joy Mott and Marilyn Taylor. 1974. vi + 31pp. (0 11 340663 0).

24.   IMPACT. Intensive matched probation and after-care treatment. Vol. I - The design of the probation experiment and an interim evaluation. M. S. Folkard, A. J. Fowles, B.C. McWilliams, W. McWilliams, D. D. Smith, D. E. Smith and G. R. Walmsley. 1974. v + 54pp. (0 11 340664 9).

25. The approved school experience. An account of boys' experiences of training under differing regimes of approved schools,with an attempt to evaluate the effectiveness of that training. Anne B. Dunlop. 1974. vii + 124pp. (0 11 340665 7).

26. Absconding from open prisons. Charlotte Banks, Patricia Mayhew and R. J. Sapsford. 1975. viii + 89pp. (0 11 340666 5).

27. Driving while disqualified. Sue Kriefman. 1975. vi + 136pp.(0 11 340667 3).

28. Some male offenders' problems. - Homeless offenders in Liverpool. W. McWilliams. II - Casework with short-term prisoners. Julie Holborn. 1975. x + 147pp. (0 11 340668 1).

29. Community service orders. K. Pease, P. Durkin, I. Earnshaw, D. Payne and J. Thorpe. 1975. viii + 80pp.(0 11 340669 X).

30. Field Wing Bail Hostel: the first nine months. Frances Simon and Sheena Wilson. 1975. viii + 55pp. (0 11 340670 3).

31. Homicide in England and Wales 1967-1971. Evelyn Gibson. 1975. iv + 59pp. (0 11 340753 X).

32. Residential treatment and its effects on delinquency. D. B. Cornish and R. V. G. Clarke. 1975. vi + 74pp. (0 11 340672 X).

33. Further studies of female offenders. Part A: Borstal girls eight years after release. Nancy Goodman, Elizabeth Maloney and Jean Davies. Part B: The sentencing of women at the London Higher Courts. Nancy Goodman, Paul Durkin and Janet Halton. Part C: Girls appearing before a juvenile court. Jean Davies. 1976. vi + 114pp. (0 11 340673 8).

34. Crime as opportunity. P. Mayhew, R. V. G. Clarke, A. Sturman and J. M. Hough. 1976. vii + 36pp.(0 11 340674 6).

35. The effectiveness of sentencing: a review of the literature. S. R. Brody. 1976. v + 89pp.(0 11 340675 4).

36. IMPACT. Intensive matched probation and after-care treatment. Vol. II - The results of the experiment. M. S. Folkard, D. E. Smith and D. D. 1976. xi + 40pp. (0 11 340676 2).

37. Police cautioning in England and Wales. J. A. Ditchfield. 1976. v + 31pp. (0 11 340677 0).

38. Parole in England and Wales. C. P. Nuttall, with E. E. Barnard, A. J. Fowles, A. Frost, W. H. Hammond, P. Mayhew, K. Pease, R. Tarling and M. J. Weatheritt. 1977. vi + 90pp. (0 11 340678 9).

39. Community service assessed in 1976. K. Pease, S. Billingham and I. Earnshaw. 1977. vi + 29pp.(0 11 340679 7).

40. Screen violence and film censorship: a review of research. Stephen Brody. 1977. vii + 179pp.(0 11 340680 0).

41. Absconding from borstals. Gloria K. Laycock. 1977. v + 82pp. (0 11 340681 9).

42. Gambling: a review of the literature and its implications for policy and research. D. B. Cornish. 1978. xii + 284pp. (0 11 340682 7).

43. Compensation orders in magistrates' courts. Paul Softley. 1978. v + 41pp. (0 11 340683 5).

44. Research in criminal justice. John Croft. 1978. iv + 16pp. (0 11 340684 3).

45. Prison welfare: an account of an experiment at Liverpool. A. J. Fowles. 1978. v + 34pp. (0 11 340685 1).

46. Fines in magistrates' courts. Paul Softley. 1978. v + 42pp. (0 11 340686 X).

47. Tackling vandalism. R. V. Clarke (editor), F. J. Gladstone, A. Sturman and Sheena Wilson 1978. vi + 91pp. (0 11 340687 8).

48. Social inquiry reports: a survey. Jennifer Thorpe. 1979. vi + 55pp. (0 11 340688 6).

49. Crime in public view. P. Mayhew, R. V. G. Clarke, J. N. Burrows, J. M. Hough and S. W. C. Winchester. 1979. v + 36pp. (0 11 340689 4).

50. Crime and the community. John Croft. 1979. v + 16pp. (0 11 340690 8).

51. Life-sentence prisoners. David Smith (editor), Christopher Brown, Joan Worth, Roger Sapsford and Charlotte Banks (contributors). 1979. iv + 51pp. (0 11 340691 6).

52. Hostels for offenders. Jane E. Andrews, with an appendix by Bill Sheppard. 1979. v + 30pp. (0 11 340692 4).

53. Previous convictions, sentence and reconviction: a statistical study of a sample of 5,000 offenders convicted in January 1971. G. J. O. Phillpotts and L. B. Lancucki. 1979. v + 55pp. (0 11 340693 2).

54. Sexual offences, consent and sentencing. Roy Walmsley and Karen White. 1979. vi + 77pp.(0 11 340694 0).

55. Crime prevention and the police. John Burrows, Paul Ekblom and Kevin Heal. 1979. v + 37pp. (0 11 340695 9).

56. Sentencing practice in magistrates' courts. Roger Tarling, with the assistance of Mollie Weatheritt. 1979. vii + 54pp. (0 11 340696 7).

57. Crime and comparative research. John Croft. 1979. iv + 16pp. (0 11 340697 5).

58. Race, crime and arrests. Philip Stevens and Carole F. Willis. 1979. v + 69pp. (0 11 340698 3).

59. Research and criminal policy. John Croft. 1980. iv + 14pp. (0 11 340699 1).

60. Junior attendance centres. Anne B. Dunlop. 1980. v + 47pp. (0 11 340700 9).

61. Police interrogation: an observational study in four police stations. Paul Softley, with the assistance of David Brown, Bob Forde, George Mair and David Moxon. 1980. vii + 67pp. (0 11 340701 7).

62. Co-ordinating crime prevention efforts. F. J. Gladstone. 1980. v + 74pp. (0 11 340702 5).

63. Crime prevention publicity: an assessment. D. Riley and P. Mayhew. 1980. v + 47pp.(0 11 340703 3).

64. Taking offenders out of circulation. Stephen Brody and Roger Tarling. 1980. v + 46pp.(0 11 340704 1).

65. Alcoholism and social policy: are we on the right lines? Mary Tuck. 1980. v + 30pp. (0 11 340705 X).

66. Persistent petty offenders. Suzan Fairhead. 1981. vi + 78pp. (0 11 340706 8).

67. Crime control and the police. Pauline Morris and Kevin Heal. 1981. v + 71pp. (0 11 340707 6).

68. Ethnic minorities in Britain: a study of trends in their position since 1961. Simon Field, George Mair, Tom Rees and Philip Stevens. 1981. v + 48pp. (0 11 340708 4).

69. Managing criminological research. John Croft. 1981. iv + 17pp. (0 11 340709 2).

70. Ethnic minorities, crime and policing: a survey of the experiences of West Indians and whites. Mary Tuck and Peter Southgate. 1981. iv + 54pp. (0 11 340765 3).

71. Contested trials in magistrates' courts. Julie Vennard. 1982. v + 32pp. (0 11 340766 1).

72 Public disorder: a review of research and a study in one inner city area. Simon Field and Peter Southgate. 1982. v + 77pp. (0 11 340767 X).

73. Clearing up crime. John Burrows and Roger Tarling. 1982. vii + 31pp. (0 11 340768 8).

74. Residential burglary: the limits of prevention. Stuart Winchester and Hilary Jackson. 1982. v + 47pp. (0 11 340769 6).

75. Concerning crime. John Croft. 1982. iv + 16pp. (0 11 340770 X).

76. The British Crime Survey: first report. Mike Hough and Pat Mayhew. 1983. v + 62pp. (0 11 340786 6).

77. Contacts between police and public: findings from the British Crime Survey. Peter Southgate and Paul Ekblom. 1984. v + 42pp. (0 11 340771 8).

78. Fear of crime in England and Wales. Michael Maxfield. 1984. v + 57pp. (0 11 340772 6).

79. Crime and police effectiveness. Ronald V Clarke and Mike Hough 1984. iv + 33pp. (0 11 340773 3).

80. The attitudes of ethnic minorities. Simon Field. 1984. v + 49pp. (0 11 3407742).

81. Victims of crime: the dimensions of risk. Michael Gottfredson. 1984. v + 54pp. (0 11 340775 0).

82. The tape recording of police interviews with suspects: an interim report. Carole Willis.1984.v + 45pp.(0 11 340776 9).

83. Parental supervision and juvenile delinquency. David Riley and Margaret Shaw. 1985.v + 90pp.(0 11 340799 8).

84. Adult prisons and prisoners in England and Wales 1970-1982: a review of the findings of social research. Joy Mott. 1985. vi + 73pp. (0 11 340801 3).

85. Taking account of crime: key findings from the 1984 British Crime Survey. Mike Hough and Pat Mayhew. 1985. vi + 115pp. (0 11 341810 2).

86. Implementing crime prevention measures. Tim Hope. 1985. vi + 82pp. (0 11 340812 9).

87. Resettling refugees: the lessons of research. Simon Field. 1985. vi + 66pp. (0 11 340815 3).

88. Investigating burglary: the measurement of police performance. John Burrows. 1986. vi + 36pp.(0 11 340824 2)

89. Personal violence. Roy Walmsley. 1986. vi + 87pp. (0 11 340827 7).

90. Police-public encounters. Peter Southgate. 1986. vi + 150pp. (0 11 340834 X).

91. Grievance procedures in prisons. John Ditchfield and Claire Austin. 1986. vi + 87pp. (0 11 340839 0).

92. The effectiveness of the Forensic Science Service. Malcolm Ramsay. 1987. v + 100pp.(0 11 340842 0).

93. The police complaints procedure: a survey of complainant's views. David Brown. 1987. v + 98pp. (0 11 340853 6).

94. The validity of the reconviction prediction score. Denis Ward. 1987. vi + 46. (0 11 340882 X).

95. Economic aspects of the illicit drug market enforcement policies in the United Kingdom. Adam Wagstaff and Alan Maynard. 1988. vii + 156pp. (0 11 340883 8)

96. Schools, disruptive behaviour and deliquency: a review of literature. John Graham. 1988. v + 70pp. (0 11 340887 0).

97. The tape recording of police interviews with suspects: a second interim report. Carole Willis, John Macleod and Peter Naish. 1988. vii + 97pp. (011 340890 0).

98. Triable-either-way cases: Crown Court or magistrate's court. David Riley and Julie Vennard. 1988. v + 52pp. (0 11 340891 9).

99. Directing patrol work: a study of uniformed policing. John Burrows and Helen Lewis. 1988 v + 66pp. (0 11 340891 9)

100. Probation day centres. George Mair. 1988. v + 44pp. (0 11 340894 3).

101. Amusement machines: dependency and delinquency. John Graham. 1988. v + 48pp. (0 11 340895 1).

102. The use and enforcement of compensation orders in magistrates' courts. Tim Newburn. 1988. v + 49pp. (0 11 340 896 X)

103. Sentencing practice in the Crown Court. David Moxon. 1988. v + 90pp. (0 11 340902 8).

104. Detention at the police station under the Police and Criminal Evidence Act 1984. David Brown. 1988. v + 88pp. (0 11340908 7).

105. Changes in rape offences and sentencing. Charles Lloyd and Roy Walmsley. 1989. vi + 53pp.(0 11 340910 9).

106. Concerns about rape. Lorna Smith. 1989. v + 48pp. (0 11 340911 7).

107. Domestic violence. Lorna Smith. 1989. v + 132pp. (0 11 340925 7)

108. Drinking and disorder: a study of non-metropolitan violence. Mary Tuck. 1989. v + 111pp. (011 340926 5).

109. Special security units. Roy Walmsley. 1989. v + 114pp. (0 11 340961 3).

110. Pre-trial delay: the implications of time limits. Patricia Morgan and Julie Vennard. 1989. v + 66pp. (0 11 340964 8)

111. The 1988 British Crime Survey. Pat Mayhew, David Elliott and Lizanne Dowds. 1989. v + 133pp. (0 11 340965 6).

112. The settlement of claims at the Criminal Injuries Compensation Board. Tim Newburn. 1989. v + 40pp. (0 11 340967 2)

113. Race, community groups and service delivery. Hilary Jackson and Simon Field. 1989. v + 62pp.(0 11 340972 9)

114. Money payment supervision orders: probation policy and practice. George Mair and Charles Lloyd. 1989.v + 40pp. (0 11 340971 0).

115. Suicide and self-injury in prison: a literature review. Charles Lloyd. 1990. v + 69pp. (0 11 3409745 5).

116. Keeping in Touch: police-victim communication in two areas. Tim Newburn and Susan Merry. 1990. v + 52pp. (0 11 340974 5).

117. The police and public in England and Wales: a British Crime Survey report. Wesley G. Skogan. 1990. vi + 74pp. (0 11 340995 8).

118. Control in prisons: a review of the literature. John Ditchfield. 1990. (0 11 340996 6).

119. Trends in crime and their interpretation: a study of recorded crime in post-war England and Wales. Simon Field. 199. (0 11 340994 X).

120. Electronic monitoring: the trials and their results. George Mair and Claire Nee. 1990. v + 79pp (0 11 340998 2).

121. Drink driving: the effects of enforcement. David Riley. 1991. viii + 78pp (0 11 340999 0).

122. Managing difficult prisoners: the Parkhurst Special Unit. Roy Walmsley (Ed.) 1991. x + 139pp (0 11 341008 5).

123. Investigating burglary: the effects of PACE. David Brown. 1991. xii + 106pp. (0 11 341011 5).

124. Traffic policing in changing times. Peter Southgate and Catriona Mirrlees-Black. 1991. viii + 139pp (0 11 341019 0)

125. Magistrates' court or Crown Court ? Mode of trial decisions and sentencing. Carol Hedderman and David Moxon. 1992. vii + 53pp. (0 11 341036 0).

126. Developments in the use of compensation orders in magistrates' courts since October 1988. David Moxon, John Martin Corkery and Carol Hedderman. 1992. x + 48pp. (0 11 341042 5).

127. A comparative study of firefighting arrangements in Britain, Denmark, the Netherlands and Sweden. John Graham, Simon Field, Roger Tarling and Heather Wilkinson. 1992. x + 57pp. (0 11 341043 3).

128. The National Prison Survey 1991: main findings. Roy Walmsley, Liz Howard and Sheila White. 1992. xiv + 82pp. (0 11 341051 4).

129. Changing the Code: police detention under the revised PACE Codes of Practice. David Brown, Tom Ellis and Karen Larcombe. 1992. viii + 122pp. (0 11 341052 2).

130. Car theft: the offender's perspective. Roy Light, Claire Nee and Helen Ingham. 1993. x + 89pp. (0 11 341069 7).

131. Housing, Community and Crime: The Impact of the Priority Estates Project. Janet Foster and Timothy Hope with assistance from Lizanne Dowds and Mike Sutton. 1993. xi + 118. (0 11 341078 6).

132. The 1992 British Crime Survey. Pat Mayhew, Natalie Aye Maung and Catriona Mirrlees-Black. 1993. xiii + 206. (0 11 341094 8).

Research and Planning Unit Papers (RPUP)

1. Uniformed police work and management technology. J. M. Hough. 1980.

2. Supplementary information on sexual offences and sentencing. Roy Walmsley and Karen White. 1980.

3. Board of visitor adjudications. David Smith, Claire Austin and John Ditchfield. 1981.

4. Day centres and probation. Suzan Fairhead, with the assistance of J.Wilkinson-Grey. 1981.

5. Ethnic minorities and complaints against the police. Philip Stevens and Carole Willis. 1982.

6. Crime and public housing. Mike Hough and Pat Mayhew (editors). 1982.

7. Abstracts of race relations research. George Mair and Philip Stevens (editors). 1982.

8. Police probationer training in race relations. Peter Southgate. 1982.

9. The police response to calls from the public. Paul Ekblom and Kevin Heal. 1982.

10. City centre crime: a situational approach to prevention. Malcolm Ramsay. 1982.

11. Burglary in schools: the prospects for prevention. Tim Hope. 1982.

12. Fine enforcement. Paul Softley and David Moxon. 1982.

13. Vietnamese refugees. Peter Jones. 1982.

14. Community resources for victims of crime. Karen Williams. 1983.

15. The use, effectiveness and impact of police stop and search powers. Carole Willis. 1983.

16. Acquittal rates. Sid Butler. 1983.

17. Criminal justice comparisons: the case of Scotland and England and Wales. Lorna J. F. Smith. 1983.

18. Time taken to deal with juveniles under criminal proceedings. Catherine Frankenburg and Roger Tarling. 1983.

19. Civilian review of complaints against the police: a survey of the United States literature. David C. Brown. 1983.

20. Police action on motoring offences. David Riley. 1983.

21. Diverting drunks from the criminal justice system. Sue Kingsley and George Mair. 1983.

22. The staff resource implications of an independent prosecution system. Peter R. Jones. 1983.

23. Reducing the prison population: an exploratory study in Hampshire. David Smith, Bill Sheppard, George Mair, Karen Williams. 1984.

24. Criminal justice system model: magistrates' courts sub-model. Susan Rice. 1984.

25. Measures of police effectiveness and efficiency. Ian Sinclair and Clive Miller. 1984.

26. Punishment practice by prison Boards of Visitors. Susan Iles, Adrienne Connors, Chris May, Joy Mott. 1984.

27. Reparation, conciliation and mediation: current projects and plans in England and Wales. Tony Marshall. 1984.

28. Magistrates' domestic courts: new perspectives. Tony Marshall (editor). 1984.

29. Racism awareness training for the police. Peter Southgate. 1984.

30. Community constables: a study of a policing initiative. David Brown and Susan Iles. 1985.

31. Recruiting volunteers. Hilary Jackson. 1985.

32. Juvenile sentencing: is there a tariff? David Moxon, Peter Jones, Roger Tarling. 1985.

33. Bringing people together: mediation and reparation projects in Great Britain. Tony Marshall and Martin Walpole. 1985.

34. Remands in the absence of the accused. Chris May. 1985.

35. Modelling the criminal justice system. Patricia M Morgan. 1985.

36. The criminal justice system model: the flow model. Hugh Pullinger. 1986.

37. Burglary: police actions and victim views. John Burrows. 1986.

38. Unlocking community resources: four experimental government small grants schemes. Hilary Jackson. 1986.

39. The cost of discriminating: a review of the literature. Shirley Dex. 1986.

40. Waiting for Crown Court trial: the remand population. Rachel Pearce. 1987.

41. Children's evidence: the need for corroboration. Carol Hedderman. 1987.

42. A preliminary study of victim offender mediation and reparation schemes in England and Wales. Gwynn Davis, Jacky Boucherat, David Watson, Adrian Thatcher (Consultant). 1987.

43. Explaining fear of crime: evidence from the 1984 British Crime Survey. Michael Maxfield. 1987.

44. Judgements of crime seriousness: evidence from the 1984 British Crime Survey. Ken Pease. 1988.

45. Waiting time on the day in magistrates' courts: a review of case listings practises. David Moxon and Roger Tarling (editors). 1988.

46. Bail and probation work: the ILPS temporary bail action project. George Mair. 1988.

47. Police work and manpower allocation. Roger Tarling. 1988.

48. Computers in the courtroom. Carol Hedderman. 1988.

49. Data interchange between magistrates' courts and other agencies. Carol Hedderman. 1988.

50. Bail and probation work II: the use of London probation/bail hostels for bailees. Helen Lewis and George Mair. 1989.

51. The role and function of police community liaison officers. Susan V Phillips and Raymond Cochrane. 1989.

52. Insuring against burglary losses. Helen Lewis. 1989.

53. Remand decisions in Brighton and Bournemouth. Patricia Morgan and Rachel Pearce. 1989.

54. Racially motivated incidents reported to the police. Jayne Seagrave. 1989.

55. Review of research on re-offending of mentally disordered offenders. David J. Murray. 1990.

56. Risk prediction and probation: papers from a Research and Planning Unit workshop. George Mair (editor). 1990.

57. Household fires: findings from the British Crime Survey 1988. Chris May. 1990.

58. Home Office funding of victim support schemes - money well spent? Justin Russell. 1990.

59. Unit fines: experiments in four courts. David Moxon, Mike Sutton and Carol Hedderman. 1990.

60. Deductions from benefit for fine default. David Moxon, Carol Hedderman and Mike Sutton. 1990.

61. Monitoring time limits on custodial remands. Paul F. Henderson. 1991.

62. Remands in custody for up to 28 days: the experiments. Paul F. Henderson and Patricia Morgan. 1991.

63. Parenthood training for young offenders: an evaluation of courses in Young Offender Institutions. Diane Caddle. 1991.

64. The multi-agency approach in practice: the North Plaistow racial harassment project. William Saulsbury and Benjamin Bowling. 1991.

65. Offending while on bail: a survey of recent studies. Patricia M. Morgan. 1992.

66. Juveniles sentenced for serious offences: a comparison of regimes in Young Offender Institutions and Local Authority Community Homes. John Ditchfield and Liza Catan. 1992.

67. The management and deployment of police armed response vehicles. Peter Southgate. 1992.

68. Using psychometric personality tests in the selection of firearms officers. Catriona Mirrlees-Black. 1992.

69. Bail information schemes: practice and effect. Charles Lloyd. 1992.

70. Crack and cocaine in England and Wales. Joy Mott (editor). 1992

71. Rape: from recording to conviction. Sharon Grace, Charles Lloyd and Lorna J.F. Smith. 1992.

72. The National Probation Survey 1990. Chris May. 1993.

73. Public satisfaction with police services. Peter Southgate and Debbie Crisp. 1993.

74. Disqualification from driving: an effective penalty? Catriona Mirrlees-Black. 1993.

75. Detention under the Prevention of Terrorism (Temporary Provisions) Act 1989: Access to legal advice and outside contact. David Brown. 1993.

76. Panel assessment schemes for mentally disordered offenders. Carol Hedderman. 1993.

77. Cash-limiting the probation service: a case study in resource allocation. Simon Field and Mike Hough. 1993.

78. The probation response to drug misuse. Claire Nee and Rae Sibbitt. 1993.

79. Approval of rifle and target shooting clubs: the effects of the new and revised criteria. John Martin Corkery. 1993.

80. The long-term needs of victims: A review of the literature. Tim Newburn. 1993.

81. The welfare needs of unconvicted prisoners. Diane Caddle and Sheila White. 1994.

82. Racially motivated crime: a British Crime Survey analysis. Natalie Aye Maung and Catriona Mirrlees-Black. 1994.

83. Mathematical models for forecasting Passport demand. Andy Jones and John MacLeod. 1994.

84. The theft of firearms. John Corkery. 1994.

85. Equal opportunities and the Fire Service. Tom Bucke. 1994.

Research Findings

(These are summaries of reports and are also available from the Information Section.)

1. Magistrates' court or Crown Court? Mode of trial decisions and their impact on sentencing. Carol Hedderman and David Moxon. 1992.

2. Surveying crime: findings from the 1992 British Crime Survey. Pat Mayhew and Natalie Aye Maung. 1992.

3. Car Theft: the offenders' perspective: Claire Nee. 1993.

4. The National Prison survey 1991: main findings. Roy Walmsley, Liz Howard and Sheila White. 1993.

5. Changing the Code: Police detention under the revised PACE codes of practice. David Brown, Tom Ellis and Karen Larcombe. 1993.

6. Rifle and pistol target shooting clubs: The effects of new approval criteria. John M Corkery. 1993.

7. Self-reported drug misuse in England and Wales. Main findings from the 1992 British Crime Survey. Joy Mott and Catriona Mirrlees-Black. 1993.

8. Findings from the International Crime Survey. Pat Mayhew. 1994.

9. Fear of Crime: Findings from the 1992 British Crime Survey. Catriona Mirrlees-Black and Natalie Aye Maung. 1994.

10. Does the Criminal Justice System treat men and women differently. Carol Hedderman and Mike Hough. 1994.

11. Participation in Neighbourhood Watch: Findings from the 1992 British Crime Survey. Lizanne Dowds and Pat Mayhew. 1994.

12. Not published yet.

13. Equal opportunities and the Fire Service. Tom Bucke. 1994.

14. Trends in Crime: Findings from the 1994 British Crime Survey. Pat Mayhew, Catriona Mirrlees-Black and Natalie Aye Maung. 1994.

Research Bulletin (available from the Information Section)

The Research Bulletin is published twice a year and consists mainly of short articles relating to projects which are part of the Home Office Research and Planning Unit's research programme.

Occasional Papers

(These can be purchased from the main Home Office Library Publications Unit, 50 Queen Anne's Gate, London SWIH 9AT. Telephone 071-273 2302 for information on price and availability. Those marked with an asterisk are out of print.)

*The 'watchdog' role of Boards of Visitors. Mike Maguire and Jon Vagg. 1984.

Shared working between Prison and Probation Officers. Norman Jepson and Kenneth Elliot. 1985.

After-care Services for Released Prisoners: A Review of the Literature. Kevin Haines. 1990.

*Arts in Prisons: towards a sense of achievement. Anne Peaker and Jill Vincent. 1990.

Pornography: impacts and influences. Dennis Howitt and Guy Cumberbatch. 1990.

*An evaluation of the live link for child witnesses. Graham Davies and Elizabeth Noon. 1991.

Mentally disordered prisoners. John Gunn, Tony Maden and Mark Swinton. 1991.

Coping with a crisis: the introduction of three and two in a cell. T G Weiler. 1992.

Psychiatric Assessment at the Magistrates' Court. Philip Joseph. 1992.

Measurement of caseload weightings in magistrates' courts. Richard J Gadsden and Graham J Worsdale. 1992.

The CDE of scheduling in magistrates' courts. John W Raine and Michael J Wilson. 1992.

Sex offenders: a framework for the evaluation of community-based treatment. Mary Barker and Rod Morgan. 1993.

Suicide attempts and self-injury in male prisons. Alison Liebling and Helen Krarup. 1993.

Measurement of caseload weightings associated with the Children's Act. Richard J Gadsden and Graham J Worsdale. 1994. (Available from the RPU Information Section).

Managing difficult prisoners: The Lincoln & Hull special units. Professor Keith Bottomley, Professor Norman Jepson, Mr Kenneth Elliott & Dr Jeremy Coid. 1994. (Available from Information Section.)

Other Books by members of RPU (available from HMSO)

Designing out crime. R. V. G. Clarke and P. Mayhew (editors). 1980. viii + 186pp.
(0 11 340732 7).

Policing today. Kevin Heal, Roger Tarling and John Burrows (editors). v + 181pp.
(0 11 340800 5).

Managing criminal justice: a collection of papers. David Moxon (editor). 1985.
vi + 222pp. (0 11 340811 0).

Situational crime prevention: from theory into practice. Kevin Heal and Gloria Laycock
(editors). 1986. vii + 166pp. (0 11 340826 9)

Communities and crime reduction. Tim Hope and Margaret Shaw (editors). 1988.
vii + 311pp. (11 340892 7).

New directions in police training. Peter Southgate (editor). 1988. xi + 256pp.
(11 340889 7).

Crime and Accountability: Victim/Offender Mediation in Practice. Tony F Marshall and
Susan Merry. 1990. xii + 262. (0 11 340973 7).

Community Work and the Probation Service. Paul Henderson and Sarah del Tufo.
1991. vi + 120. (0 11 341004 2).

Part Time Punishment? George Mair. 1991. 258 pp. (0 11 340981 8).

Analysing Offending. Data, Models and Interpretations. Roger Tarling. 1993.
viii + 203. (0 11 341080 8).

Printed in the United Kingdom for HMSO
Dd297399 11/94 C10 G559 10170